T0289712

ROUTLEDGE LIBRARY EDITIONS:
MANAGEMENT

Volume 28

# THE CULTURE OF
# MONOPOLY MANAGEMENT

# THE CULTURE OF
# MONOPOLY MANAGEMENT

## An Interpretive Study in an American Utility

STEVEN P. FELDMAN

LONDON AND NEW YORK

First published in 1986 by Garland Publishing, Inc.

This edition first published in 2018
by Routledge
2 Park Square, Milton Park, Abingdon, Oxon OX14 4RN

and by Routledge
711 Third Avenue, New York, NY 10017

*Routledge is an imprint of the Taylor & Francis Group, an informa business*

*British Library Cataloguing in Publication Data*
A catalogue record for this book is available from the British Library

ISBN: 978-1-138-55938-7 (Set)
ISBN: 978-1-351-05538-3 (Set) (ebk)
ISBN: 978-0-8153-9323-8 (Volume 28) (hbk)
ISBN: 978-1-351-18907-1 (Volume 28) (ebk)

**Publisher's Note**
The publisher has gone to great lengths to ensure the quality of this reprint but points out that some imperfections in the original copies may be apparent.

**Disclaimer**
The publisher has made every effort to trace copyright holders and would welcome correspondence from those they have been unable to trace.

THE CULTURE OF
MONOPOLY MANAGEMENT ★ An Interpretive Study
in an American Utility

Steven P. Feldman

Garland Publishing, Inc.
New York & London ★ 1986

**Library of Congress Cataloging-in-Publication Data**

Feldman, Steven P. (Steven Paul), 1954–
  The culture of monopoly management.

  (American business history)
  Thesis (Ph.D.)—University of Pennsylvania, 1982.
  Bibliography: p.
  Includes Index.
  1. American Telephone and Telegraph Company—
Management—History.  2. Telephone—United States—
Management—History.  I. Title.  II. Series.
HE8846.A55F4  1986      384.6'065'73      86-9937
ISBN 0-8240-8376-8

All volumes in this series are printed on acid-free,
250-year-life paper.

Printed in the United States of America

TABLE OF CONTENTS

Charts

# Chapter I

## MANAGEMENT AS A CULTURAL SYSTEM

### I.  Introduction

The objectives of this research are twofold:  one, the primary objective is to provide a detailed description of the cultural aspects of interpersonal relationships as they are found in the career development process and the cooperative process; two, to develop a theory of culture and apply it to these parts of a modern organization.  The focus will be on the parts of the culture that have to do with the categories that are used by managers to protect and advance their careers and to initiate and contribute to collective effort.

Access to these perceptions and processes was gained through an analysis of discourse used by informants to describe these perceptions and processes and through the observations of individuals acting within these contexts.  The top forty-eight managers of an American utility was the group that was chosen for study.  This includes a CEO, ten vice-presidents, and thirty-seven assistant vice-presidents.  This group was chosen because of the lack of empirical data on the specific day-to-day work life of monopoly managers in the literature on organizations.  The top levels were chosen because these individuals were the successful ones who were best able to adapt to the demands of a monopoly environment, thus most clearly reflecting the monopoly culture we were interested in studying.

This particular utility is a telephone utility.  And in 1981, when the fieldwork was carried out, the telephone system was preparing to be broken up.  Thus, the end of an era, which began at the end of World

1

War II and developed into the 1980s, was the context of this research. It was becoming apparent that the managers were no longer adequately trained for the tasks they were now beginning to face. And the processes that had provided the training were being called into question. They represented an era when this telephone utility was not under financial pressure because of legal protection from a government mandate to provide universal service and from the tremendous cost savings resulting from technological breakthroughs originating at Bell Labs. Hence, this study focuses on the culture of interpersonal relations in a monopoly organization that had historically been financially secure and legally protected. And even though they were entering a period of change, their practices had not changed in any considerable amount, since the monopoly, in 1981, still maintained monopoly conditions of trade.

The general theoretical position that is being applied to this context can be stated in the form of a hypothesis. It is that the culture of interpersonal relations is the central category of organizational cultures. By central I mean that the categories that are used by managers to evaluate other managers for competence, trust, reliability, influence, personableness, etc. are the most often used in general and are most often used in situations that are deemed important. Thus, it is proposed here that this study of interpersonal relations is a picturing of the heart of this organizational culture. Career development and cooperation were chosen as the processes to best represent interpersonal relationships because they proved to be central to managerial interaction over the eight months of fieldwork.

Now the interpretive proposition that the categories for inter-personal relationships are the heart of organizational cultures cannot be proven in the sense of an experiment. What we will be doing here is building a case with this proposition in mind and will have to appraise the description of the cultural aspects of the career development process and the cooperative process in the conclusion to see if a strong case has been made. It will be a statement made, an empirical contribution, it will have to battle with future empirical studies before its validity can be more deeply specified.

One last point should be made before beginning the discussion on the theoretical framework. In doing cultural studies the researcher should be trained to eliminate or control his own cultural inclinations from distorting the final description of the culture of the group studied. Normally a difficult task, when studying one's own culture it becomes increasingly difficult. The problem is somewhat reduced when studying American "culture" because it is so various it really cannot be pinned down to a consistent group of categories. Thus, when, for example, a business student raised in a Jewish family in Cleveland studies a Spanish community in Los Angeles, he witnesses many new styles of life. Nonetheless, there will usually be an overlap of shared cultural categories that will be difficult for the researcher to recognize, let alone step out of.

In this situation there will be a tendency for the researcher to use the categories in his own perceptions and research actions, thus limiting his ability to expose the categories of his informants. I think this is somewhat inevitable in studying one's own culture and can only be eliminated altogether by having multiple studies by multiple people, then the comparative sweep should eliminate much of the bias or blind spots. I admit to this phenomena being active in this research and feel it appropriate to state at the beginning that this cultural study is influenced to a degree by my opinions and past experiences. In this regard I would recommend to the reader the fourth section of this chapter where I have tried to state a self-examination in relation to the concept of management which I use in this research.

## II. A General Theory of Action

The study of modern organizations has taken many forms. Major contemporary paradigms rely heavily on structural or functional, or some combination of the two, approaches. Both functional and structural emphasis in the study of social systems have their advantages. But as sure as they show strengths they also show weaknesses. Neither approach has been successful in dealing with cultural and social processes on an equal basis. One concept always becomes secondary. Either culture is derived sociologically or social organization is derived from culture. An example of the former reductionism is the explanation of racial preferences, a cultural factor, wholly in terms of its functional value to increase conformity in order to maintain predictability and trust.[1] An example of the latter reductionism is explaining conformity wholly in terms of a "moral imperative," ignoring demographic and technological influences.[2]

Another concern about the study of the modern organization is that it is a bit like reporting on a fire; the events are happening so fast and unpredictably that one cannot anticipate or prepare for observation. This rapid flow of unpredictable events can be summed up in one word, change. But just what is changing? Is it social structure or cultural system or both? Social structure is the concretized "things" in the world and culture is the import we attribute to these things. They are both analytic abstractions from the same one world. Therefore, when we speak of a changing environment we are speaking about changes in both analytic systems, since if one is changing the other must also, since they are both in the one "there" together. With this said, however, it does not follow that they change in a harmonious or balanced way.

One way of viewing the relation between culture and social structure is to see culture as an ordered group of meaningful forms (symbols) in terms of which social action takes place, and to see social structure as the pattern of social activity itself.[3] Even though they are separable conceptually, culture and social structure combine in a specific event in any one of many possible integrations. Hence, change can be seen to come about through the process of integration of the cultural and structural systems when one is incongruent with the other. It is the discontinuities between culture and social structure that are fundamentally responsible for change. Nonchange can then be seen as just one position in a range of modes of integration where the two analytic systems are not in conflict.

Change, then, is the result of a lack of integration between social structure and culture. The lack of integration comes about through the independent aspect of the relationship between culture and social structure. The independence is based on two different types of integration that each system performs.[4] Culture is characterized by "logico-meaningful integration." Social structure is characterized by "causal-functional integration." Again, though, if one changes they both change because they are interdependent.

Logico-meaningful integration, characteristic of culture, refers to a process that seeks a unity of meaning. This process takes two semantic wholes and forms them into a single whole. For example, a monopoly manager integrating his traditional conception of management (no decision is better than a wrong decision) with his new awareness (if I do not do something my competitor will take over my market share); and as will be shown below the obvious integration of these two differing orientations is not obvious at all.

Causal-functional integration, characteristic of social structure, is the kind of integration the monopoly manager would make if he started making decisions and taking actions based on incomplete information. Under monopoly conditions he simply waited for near certainty before taking actions. In a competitive environment he does not have this option. If in a competitive environment he evaluates the market demand, realizes its ambiguity, but guesses as to what general pattern is at work and implements his product strategy accordingly, then he has integrated his practices to function in the new social structure.

It is because these two types of integration are different (did the manager's product strategy fail because risk meant danger rather than opportunity or because his product hit the market too late?) that there is an inherent incongruity and tension between the two systems. Hence, all types of social action must be understood by weaving together a picture of the multiple meanings of social reality.

In addition to social and cultural systems the general theory of action postulates a third independent yet interdependent system, personality, common to all social action. The personality concept enables the analysis of the individual's motivational style to be carried out. And then by relating the personality data back to the general framework, the intimate relationship between culture and personality is analyzed. For example, in Chapter III an individual that had an independent character found his career frozen and had to quit because of his inability to be accepted into a context of conformity.

The independence of the personality system rests on the unique history of the individual. Because of physical structure, biological needs, and cultural background (e.g. child rearing, education) the individual will always be involved in an attempt to integrate, within his own recognition, his tendencies and ambitions. Even though culture and social structure both stimulate and limit the individual, he claims his own private existence through the uniqueness of his individual history. The typological study of common character traits found in any society never exhausts the variability of character traits in that society. Hence, an accurate study of social action must do better than claim to have sketched out the common character traits of individuals involved in that action, it must describe the specific characters involved in that action. Only in this way can the boundries of cultural categories in service during these actions be drawn and the actual functioning of personalities within those cultural categories be studied.

Thus because of this interdependent nature of the three components in social action, change in the whole system can originate in any one component. Change is caused by one system developing in a way that puts it in conflict with another system. At Bell the idea "service" provides the Bell employee with much of his corporate sense of self. This cultural aspect of his action is now incongruent with the court ruling which radically changes his structural relations to the marketplace. It demands that his actions be guided fundamentally by return on investment rather than quality of service to the customer. In many situations the Bell employee is confounded because he knows his traditional orientation is not appropriate to guide his actions to accomplish new company goals. Either the court will have to reverse its ruling or the corporate culture will have to change and the individual's managerial style along with it.

Within this general theory of action the primary focus will be on the cultural aspects of social action. The reason for this is that the cultural aspects of modern organizations have been the least studied, and because it is a general hypothesis of this research that culture plays the key role in managerial processes. The system of guiding principles (symbolic codes) used by any group will be the main influence for choosing the mode of social organization and for the interpersonal dynamics within that organization. It is by studying the cultural aspects of its economic organizations that management in the United States can gain the knowledge to reeducate its workers and redesign its organizations in order to operate efficiently and humanly in a changing world.

III. An Interpretive Theory of Culture

The interpretive theory of culture rests on a semiotic concept of culture. Semiotics is the study of symbols. A symbol is a meaning that represents another meaning. In the statement, "The new sales strategies are being carried out by the marketing shop," shop symbolizes a physical location and an area of responsibility, even though its literal meaning denotes a small retail outlet or a craftsman's place of work. Thus, the semiotic approach posits social action as symbolic action. In attempting to explain social action as symbolic action we are essentially dealing with meaning.

Meaning denotes intention. The meaning being cognized by an individual when he expresses himself is the significance of his statement in relation to his self-understanding. When the individual expresses a meaning he intends to say something in relation to other meanings that constitute his conceptual universe. Hence, symbolic action is an expression of self through the service of meanings that constitute the individual's awareness.

Now, we must seek the source of this conceptual universe that the individual has access to and uses for the purpose of framing the meanings that he wishes to express. It is here that we can make sense out of the concept of symbolic action. The answer is that this conceptual universe is culture. Mind is predominantly public because meaning is. As we say above, meaning is carried through the service of symbols. Symbols are historically developed, socially maintained, and individually applied. We know that symbols are historically developed, for we can trace the development of their meaning through their uses in different contexts over time. If symbols are historically developed, then they must be passed on from generation to generation. This process would rule out any private theory of mind, since knowledge must be able to be independently checked for it to be knowledge, and since an individual with a private symbol could not pass it on because he would have no independent way to know what he was passing on.[5] Therefore, symbols are socially maintained, since only then can meaning be checked for truth and thus knowledge somewhat controlled.

Culture, then, is an acted text that is collectively written. This text, these meanings, are the socially established conceptual structures in terms of which the members of the collectivity signal to one another, interpret one another's signals, and act toward one another. Thus, culture is not only public but also it is ideational. It is ideational because of its metaphysical use.

In regarding it as a text, one must be careful not to imagine an organized systematic body of knowledge. The many parts of social life all have their cultural significance, but the various symbolic structures representing these parts of social life fit together in not necessarily a harmonious or logical manner. Since these symbol systems are historically developed, and since new social phenomena are always swimming into view in need of symbolic notation the various symbol systems will be different ages and thus different levels of development and integration. Hence, what the student of cultural study is faced with is interworked systems of construable symbols. Interworked can be imagined as a multiple of ropes, some knotted, some not, all knotted together into a vast jumble of form. This totality of forms, each one

having its own nature, combine into a somewhat sensible somewhat contradictory form, which is the culture of the organization.

None-the-less, many cultural categories are directly related to
others, and indeed some are dependent on others for their meaning.
Thus, in an unmachine-like way the management group is involved in a
"cultural system." But before going on and stating the properties of a
"system," it must be noted that modern society is comprised of individuals making cultural attachments on many levels. Not only because
individuals in modern society have "private" lives that have little to
do with their professional lives, but because different cultural categories exist on different levels of generalization. And individuals
can make primary attachments at different levels.[6] Among the forty-
eight managers studied at this company, four different primary attachments can be discerned: self-centered attachments (primary interest in
one's own wants), interpersonal attachments (e.g. attachments to one's
boss), attachments to the organization, and attachments to the parent
company. Furthermore, the more general attachments (e.g., to the
parent company) were no less enthusiastic than the personal attachments
to one's self or one's boss.

With this in mind the idea of a "cultural system" becomes a loose
cover term for a field of problematic cooperative activity based on
control mechanisms that are more or less integrated. It is the precise
task of the cultural theorist to specify just what the more or less
amounts to in any particular case. And to carry out this task, the concept of system is quite valuable. The concept of system has five
components:[7] a system must have parts, the parts taken together

constitute a whole within which their presence is logical, their inter-relationships motivated, and their workings comprehensible. The constraints are partial, the logic approximate, the motivations incomplete, and the comprehensibility limited, thus the system is never fully coherent. But, however imperfect, the organization of cultural categories into an ordered whole with its own properties and dynamics is real. It can be described as a cultural system, and once described it can extend our understanding of how a management group operates and why.

In studying these symbolic structures one looks for the general pattern of behavior, since culture is public it is shared. It is through social behavior that culture is articulated. The cognitive means used by the individual to maintain the use of his culture has been called partial equivalence structures.[8] The individual of the collectivity recognizes that the behavior of others under various circumstances is predictable and thus can be predictably related to his own actions. Culture, then, from the individual's perspective, is a set of standardized models which facilitate contractual relationships in which the equivalent roles are specified and available for use by any two members of the social system. So we see that though the conceptual universe that the individual operates within is public he need not share all cognitions or perceptions of reality with other members of the social system, but only shares cultural patterns that he and other community members use to organize their behavior. The individual, in a sense, does have a private world which is unique to him. All his cognitions are not shared, but he need only share certain cognitions with his fellow community members to act effectively and acceptably as a member of the group. Where the complementarity starts to get vague, we begin to leave culture and arrive at the uniqueness of personality. This is also the area where interpersonal understanding begins to grow weak because individual action becomes less guided by shared cultural categories than by impulses not clearly understood even by the individual himself. And since only individual action can be observed this culture-personality crossroads becomes the focal point of analysis, since it is here that the researcher, rooted in personality, can study culture, or rooted in culture, can study personality.

Thus, culture is public, systemic, ideational, and found in social action. Social action was said to be seen as symbolic action. For us symbolic action is the cultural meanings that the individual is suspended by in his realtion to reality. Thus, culture is context. Culture is the socially maintained and individually applied set of circumstances that surround a particular situation being lived by the individuals involved in that situation. The individual uses culture by making use of cultural categories to organize his understanding and behavior. We must now unpack the meaning of the word "use." How does the individual use culture?

The individual uses culture to make sense out of social phenomena by categorizing them. Some new event or individual is understood by relating the new qualities to one's past experiences. This is the interpretive approach. A Bell manager heard that another manager was being sent to a management seminar. He disclosed to himself that the phrase "going to a management seminar" meant, in this context, that the manager involved was being considered for promotion. He came to this conclusion through the use of previously developed categories by appropriating the new information into a broader context constructed by these categories. That is, he made an interpretation of an event.

Interpretation is an inductive process. Induction is a process of reasoning in which a general conclusion is reached from a specific statement. In our illustration the Bell manager reached the general conclusion that another manager was being considered for a promotion from the specific event of being told that a manager was being sent to a management seminar.

Exactly the same method is used by the student of culture to make sense out of the behavior that he observes.[9] So we see that if a researcher was told by an informant of our Bell manager's interpretation of his peer the researcher would necessarily make an interpretation of an interpretation—in order to understand it. This is so because the researcher would have to bring it home, so to speak, to his own experiential frame.

For heuristic purposes the interpretive approach can be seen as having four steps. As we have said, it is inductive and thus its momentum is to go from a particular to a general. The mechanics of this "going" begins with guessing. Geertz calls this the use of presumptive signifiers.[10] Presumptive is a probable (deemed probable) guess that is open to debate on its validity. Signifier is an object that expresses meaning. This is where the interpretive approach begins: in a mad scramble for the vaguest understanding. This first guess is a description that is directed by a theory that provides it with its conceptual force. Theory and description are hand in hand through the entire interpretive process.

The second step is the assessment of the guess. This is done by checking the guess in relation to other sources of information. For example, the Bell manager might check the curriculum of the seminar to see if the level of education is relevant to the job that the manager would be doing if he were promoted to the next level above his present level.

In the third step, the interpreter attempts to "thickly" describe the object of his inquiry. The Bell manager first guessed that his peer's seminar assignment was a step towards promotion and then checked this by another source of information. He might then begin to thicken his description of his peer's context by interpreting that the manager was being groomed for a new opening in the organizational redesign that called for an individual with a marketing background and a knowledge of computers. Further, the manager's new practice of coming early and staying late could now be better understood in this context: somebody is watching. Thus step three, what Geertz calls "thick description,"[11] is a procedure to frame the reality by giving it certain meanings that were theoretically derived from historically developed categories. The theory referred to here would be something about the nature of the relationships between promotions and education and presentation of self and organizational redesign.

Finally, we come to the fourth step where the interpretive approach reaches its destination, diagnosis. Diagnosis is a more advanced form of description (than step three) that attempts to charterize precisely;

whereas, in the third step, the description was of a specific action it is here attempting to become general. The object of diagnosis is to broaden out the system of analysis that is implicit in the thick description. The diagnostician wants to know what the knowledge gained in the thick description demonstrates about the individual beyond the context or what the knowledge demonstrates beyond the individual and about his culture in general or even about all individuals and all cultures. The Bell manager could, perhaps, induce that his peer was planning to make a large purchase and needed a better income statement to get the loan. Or that most Bell managers were attempting to position themselves to benefit from the new organizational structure and the future Bell employee would be aggressive and ambitious rather than dedicated and loyal. Hence, diagnosis seeks a deeper cause or nature for explanation of the thickly described behavior.

The interpretive approach is used to reach generalizations by generalizing within a case (as done above) rather than generalizing across many cases. Generalizing within a case is done by approaching the inquiry in a microscopic mode, that is, approaching small matters (forty-eight managers). Once a small social system is chosen precise detailed observations are made over a prolonged period of time. The generalizations come about through the delicacy of distinctions made by the observer. Delicacy refers to the fineness of perceptions of reality. These small facts speak to large issues (individuals to organizations) because specifics lay the foundations for generalizations. The important thing about the findings from this approach is their complex specificness. This is where the high level theory gets its sensible actuality without which it is vacuous. Sensible means perceived by the senses and actuality refers to the existence we live. It is here, in the concrete situation, that our concepts and theories find their creative and imaginative force. Small facts speak to large issues because we make them. If they help us understand then the generalization is valid until a better one comes along.

The student of culture uses the interpretive approach in studying the culture's symbolic structures in order to be able to explain what role culture plays in that social system. He wants to know how a particular culture makes a contruction of--puts a form on--the collective life. In our over-used example, the Bell manager puts a form on his peer's situation by using his cultural understanding that resulted in interpreting an action about his fellow manager's training into an upward mobility, rather than lateral mobility, or any other, context. It is the object of this research to gather together these threads of understanding, locate their interconnections, and portray the way of life that is at stake in them.

IV.  A Concept of Management

Management is a form of social action. It is a form that is generated when a hierarchical structure is set up for the purpose of organizing work effort in order to accomplish collective ends. The manager is the individual within this structure who has responsibility for directing other managers or non-managerial workers. Management is the practices and conduct that managers carry out when guiding others in their work. This definition brings into focus the interpersonal factors in management. An accountant, for example, would not be a manager unless his numbers led him to make decisions that directed the work of others.

To understand the data that this definition of management will direct us towards, we will need to design a concept of management that will be able to analyze the data through general categories. The concept of management that will be employed here will have sociological, economic, and psychological categories shaping its interpretive structure.

Since the data was mostly collected through participant observation, and since this is an empirical study attempting to explore the cultural significance of action, it is advantageous, here, to discuss the meaning of the three categories giving body to the concept of management in a personal way. That is, to merge the conceptual training the researcher has had within those concepts with his past research experiences and other relevant experiences that will shed light on the meaning he gives those categories. This will enable the reader to have an understanding of the researcher, thus enabling the reader to better understand the context of this research.

The three categories of the concept of management will be represented by three subconcepts. They are the concepts of authority, uncertainty, and the unconscious. The concept of authority is the most recent major addition to the way I see the world and my place in it. Its lateness no doubt is a signal to the state of my maturational development and a signal of the confused state of our educational institutions. For some of us the rebellion of adolesence does not peak in the early and mid-teens, but continues into later life. Due to certain anti-social attitudes on my part and the cultural reinforcement of these attitudes, in general, in the 1960s and early 1970s, and the ability to study social organization in the social science departments in American universities without having to confront the concept, it was possible to ignore or sidestep the primary role of authority in understanding social processes. Indeed, my early interest in Marxian economics in 1976, at the end of my undergraduate education and the beginning of my graduate, was based more on an implicit assumption that the present authority was corrupt and in need of attack than it was a search for a new authority.

The contemporary "problem of authority" is a result of the weakening of the moral power of religious systems and the increasing influence of rational explanatory systems for understanding the world. As Nietzsche has pointed out, the problem lies in the inability of science or rationalistic and idealistic philosophy to provide the ends for which we live: Ends can never be proven to be correct, but instead are ultimately based on faith. In the latter half of the twentieth century a considerable number of people have, despite early predictions about "the death of God," kept their faith. But for others, the majority, a nausia, an alienation, a skepticism, a neurosis, has taken hold as an expression of the felt inner confusion and outer fear. Kafka's entire life's work, for example, was a painful attempt to find guiding principles in a world where principles were supposed to be based on reason rather than faith. Leading American intellectuals have taken up this problem and to this day keep offering syntheses or new models to provide direction to a misdirected populace. Robert Bellah's, a Berkeley sociologist, work Beyond Belief is both a clear and current example of this phenomenon. With teenage suicide up three hundred percent over the last twenty-five years we can be sure that the problem of belief is not leaving us in the last half of the twentieth century.[12]

It was within this general context that I took a class with the sociologist Philip Rieff, in the fall of 1980. It was a seminar and the text used was Max Weber's "Politics as a Vocation." Under Professor Rieff's teaching methods and Weber's brilliant work I started to see the central importance of the concept of authority in all social organization. My sensitivity to the subordinate's deference signalling as it plays a role in his career development was opened up by this concept, for example. The three types of authority that Weber postulated— traditional, charismatic, and legal—is a general framework that is used to help locate this management structure in its historical context. I conclude early on in this thesis that Americans (and I find specification in the managers of this utility) are primarily responsive to charismatic authority. Indeed, the general nature of authority that is

demonstrated in each chapter and is responsible for the general managerial orientation is a belief in the personal qualities of individuals
as they are wrapped in the formal authority of office. This idea of
"institutional charisma" is theoretically elaborated in "Charisma,
Order, and Status," an important essay by Edward Shils.

The second concept that is an important guide for my understanding
of social organization is the concept of uncertainty and with it the
concept of risk. I formed these concepts at a very young age due to
exposure to an entrepreneur father. My father, his brothers, and a
brother-in-law managed a family-owned wholesale produce company. It
is the kind of business where one attempts to buy low and sell high,
and do all this rather quickly before the fruits and vegetables lose
their color, their hardness, their smell, and ultimately their consuma-
bility. My observation of my father's business practices is clearly
the biggest influence on my understanding of the meaning of management.
And his work in a risky industry where supply and demand are a constantly
fluxuating phenomenon was the first reason I saw dealing with uncertainty as the fundamental program of management.

In addition, my undergraduate and graduate training in economics
heightened this sensibility. In 1977 I read Frank H. Knight's classic
in economic theory Risk, Uncertainty, and Profit. At this point I
started to develop a theoretical understanding of entrepreneurship and
the capacities that are needed to deal with uncertainty. At about
the same time I read Joseph Shumpeter's great work Capitalism, Socialism, and Democracy and another of his important works The Theory of
Economic Development. This reinforced my understanding of risk and

uncertainty as being center stage in economic development and their being the primary reasons for the mode of managerial organization that is adopted.

In 1979 I was hired by a research center at the Wharton School of Finance and Commerce to study the apparel industry. I began this project by interviewing the presidents of forty apparel companies. Most of the apparel companies were small family run firms, many of which were of Jewish background (similar to my own family). I worked with a number of these firms over an eighteen month period and got to know about management styles and practices in the apparel industry. Profits in the apparel industry, on a national average, were about one and a half percent of sales. This extremely competitive industry was filled with uncertainty and risk. Fashions, it seemed to me, were anybody's guess each season. The result of this experience was to further develop my understanding of risk and uncertainty and their influence on managerial styles and economic organization.

This understanding plays a major role throughout this thesis. When I arrived at this utility and found decision avoidance and risk aversive management styles, it clearly did not fit into the category of entrepreneurship that was my central means to understand management. I was faced with the task of working through this data to find a way to bring it into my self-understanding. Participant observation was an important tool for this working through. As I became a participant in this social system I began to be subjected to the same pressures and processes that the managers, whose styles I was interested in studying, were. In this situation, a new situation for me, I did not know how to act or protect myself and was quickly looking around for models and advice. In this way, life in a large bureaucracy started to become apparent to me. And with this data in mind, my final interpretation of my experiences was primarily shaped by the collision of an image of openly aggressive, fast moving, self-confident entrepreneurs with the slow moving, decision avoiding, self-protecting monopoly managers.

The last concept I deem central to my intellectual approach is the concept of the unconscious—meanings active but barred from cognition. My first exposure to the concept was Irving Stone's biography of Sigmund Freud, Passions of the Mind. This was in 1974 and I have been a reader of Freud, Klein, Erikson, and other psychoanalytic theorists since. In addition I have been involved in psychoanalytic therapy. Even though the involvement had been for personal reasons, the intellectual impact has been considerable. As I learned to seek deeper or other meanings to my own actions, I began doing so for others; as I began to know that I was not the captain of my own ship I began to assume others were not in total control either. As I began to realize the tremendous impact childhood had on my present perception and wants, I began to see childhood as the primary force on character development. After studying Freud's three models of the mind I started becoming sensitive to language as the carrier of reality. As Susan Sontag has recently written in an essay on French literary critic Roland Barthes, "Language is everything."[13] And even noting the exaggeration involved in this proposition, I still look to language for my most primordial relation to the world.

The unconscious as Freud found it in language (and called it the "primary process" with cognition being "secondary") was just one more devastating blow to the idea of objectivity. Marx with his idea of "historical forces" at work in the individual, Nietzsche with his "glosses on the will to power" are two other examples of the attack on the "thing in itself." The message is: Reality has been decentered. We can never be certain about any knowledge: Meaning is multiple and always open to multiple interpretations. Twentieth century philosophy parallels these conclusions. Heidegger's theory of art as a creative tension between "world" and "earth" never allows one to arrive at the "essence" of the work of art, its one true meaning.[14] Or Wittgenstein's idea of language games clearly moves the focus of reality on to words and their relationships. He points us towards the language we use to describe something, if we want to know it better.[15]

All this high talk about the unconscious and its medium in language use has its effect in this study of management by a distrust of the said. The said becomes a voice heard from, an opinion collected, but the meaning attributed to the said is held back, it is held up to different theoretical lights, it is twisted about to attempt to understand it from many different angles. The researcher becomes suspicious of language itself, suspicious that an uncontrolled, implicit meaning is lurking somewhere on the surface of a sentence. He becomes suspicious not only of the said but of himself (the heard). It demands patience on the part of the researcher. He has to be patient to observe the pattern of his own inclinations and patient to observe the same individuals over an extended period of time doing the same things in order that the consistent patterns can be perceived.

Also, the concept of the unconscious has a considerable influence on the concept of culture. In the previous section it was stated that a semiotic concept of culture posits a public theory of mind; that is, mind as a set of public symbolic codes. But if this concept of culture is allowed to exhaust the meaning of the conceptual category of mind, then the result is that personality is reduced to a cultural symbol (this is similar to the sociological reduction of culture mentioned earlier). Thus, the concept of the unconscious defends a certain conceptual territory for the belief in individual uniqueness to survive along side the belief that man is a cultural animal. The concept of culture is held in a tension, never quite able to claim total control over man's mental life. In this sense I move away from Geertz's view of culture as a public mind and closer to Wallace's view of culture as a set of shared contractual agreements. Regardless of the precise theortical boundry, however, this thesis is fundamentally carried out by the simultaneous basing in one side of the culture--personality framework while exploring and speculating about the other. As Geertz has said:

> "We must, in short, descend into detail, past the
> misleading tags, past the metaphysical types, past
> the empty similarities to grasp firmly the essen-
> tial character of not only the various cultures
> but the various sorts of individuals within each
> culture, if we wish to encounter humanity face to
> face."[16]

And since culture is shared, it therefore means that cultural theorists must spend a good deal, the majority, of their time doing detailed examinations of the individual. In this way the leap to culture is made.

With these three subconcepts structuring the concept of management, we collected and analyzed the data on monopoly management. Thus, the authority concept directed the research towards power relations between the levels of hierarchy and amongst managers on the same level. Also, our authority concept made us sensitive to forms of obedience. The uncertainty concept directed us toward decision making and modes for the gathering and manipulating of information. A background in entre- preneurial research brought leadership roles and leadership styles into center stage as they influenced organizational processes. Lastly, the concept of the unconscious made us acutely interested in discourse. Words became important as carriers of what Ricoeur called "surplus meaning."[17] Furthermore, it led us toward the meaning that is concealed behind what is revealed in all cultural categories. Above all, manage- ment is a cultural phenomenon, and culture not only lightens some paths, it also darkens others.

V.   Data Collection in Fieldwork Methods

Now that the higher levels of theory have been discussed we arrive at their application in fieldwork methods. As was stated above, the primary method of data collection was participant observation. Participant observation, however, can mean a great many things. I will use the term to mean researcher-informant interactions where both parties are actively engaged in explaining their thoughts to the other and understanding the thoughts of the other. This somewhat intellectualized definition of participant observation focuses primary attention on the discussions that took place during the various kinds of interviews that were conducted. It was here, in the one-on-one situation, that much of the data that was used in this ethnographic report was collected. Also, lunches, dinners, and out for drinks were excellent opportunities to gather information. In these situations notes would have to be written up as soon after the event took place as possible.

My style of participant observation was a direct personal involvement in the lives of the managers I was interested to, and was permited to, study. When I went to meet an individual I attempted to find out what was important to him. For the first two months I only asked two questions: one, what is the current situation the organization is in; and two, what role do you play in the organization. These very general questions stimulated a variety of answers. But each answer expressed an idea of what that individual felt to be the pressing concerns of the present situation. Some got off on tangents about their army unit some thirty years ago or their high school athletic accomplishments some forty years ago, but no matter what they discussed I assumed it in some way reflected on their current situation. And it was my job to find out in what way it did so.

I tried to engage them--question them, ask for elaborations, details, examples--in the areas they felt inclined to discuss. Sometimes I felt that their discussion was concealing more than it was attempting to clarify and I would attempt to change the subject. If a new subject still was phrased in what I felt to be platitudes, I would argue with their conclusions and perceptions. The technique of disagreeing with informants was a most valuable tool for getting at sensitive and important data. Most managers had a fairly high opinion of their ability to understand the corporation and when this opinion was challenged it usually brought out their best, most clear explanation of the organization and their place in it. None-the-less, if an individual persisted in talking about a certain aspect of corporate life I did not deem important, I usually allowed (I did not leave) the individual to complete his story. Sometimes these "irrelevant" stories turned out to be important later on.

My better and more valuable relationships were ones where a friendship had developed. In some cases managers had children close to my age and involved in graduate or professional schools. These managers were quick to take a positive attitude towards me and eager to help me with my research. They were quick to understand my motivation and my situation. In these cases their friendship was based on a parental affection. Other kinds of friendships were based on personal respect. These relationships evolved as we got to know each other and were attracted to each other's outlook, integrity, generosity, or intellect.

These were clearly the strongest bonds I made during the fieldwork and some have turned into lasting friendships that are active today--ten months after the fieldwork has ended. From these friendships I got the most systematic, sensitive data. Because of the level of trust that was maintained, I was able to get "confidential" data about private relationships and embarrasing events. Even though I was not able to use this highly personal data in the ethnography, it did influence the pattern model that was developed, but less personal data was used to portray it.

Within these more general comments, three kinds of interviews can be discerned. First, the structured interviews were used to get demographic data and personal history. Sixteen of these interviews were conducted, thirteen on the AVP level and three on the VP level. Each interview took about three hours. Second were the open or free floating interviews which were to a degree based on free association on both my part and the informant's part. Almost invariably I arrived for an interview with a topic of interest and started out with questions that built up to this topic. If the manager was suspicious or if I was insecure I began with a review of my research. Sometimes this review led to the informant's own opinions by adding to my perceptions or disagreeing with them. Anyway, the dialogue was not explicitly structured and can be best described as a floating negotiation as to which issues were mutually deemed important.

The third type of interview (which perhaps could be better described as a meeting to gather information) was one where no notes were immediately taken. These situations came about during meetings where I could not take notes (e.g., lunches), where I was tired and could not write any longer, where it was asked to be off the record (in which case it was never written down), and with individuals who were uncomfortable with the note taking and thus I felt a better discussion could be had without it. In these cases I was better positioned to watch eye and body movements and informant reactions to my own statements and responses. These interactions were less formal and usually developed into: one, being offered the role of a sympathetic listener, which I usually accepted; or two, an intellectual relationship based on back and forth discussion of views on particular issues.

Outside of the participant observation there were meetings that were attended without any participation on my part other than my being there (which, even though managers usually denied it, seemed to have an affect on group process). Most of the meetings were formal groups that met on a regular basis. Even though I took "copious" notes at these meetings, much of my notes were discussions of technical matters that were difficult to understand. It turned out that more was learned from what did not go on in these meetings rather than what did (e.g., almost no conflict). It was valuable, however, to see which individuals were feared or respected, since these observations sometimes differed from what I was told in confidence (e.g., almost none of the staff AVPs accurately described the extent of influence one line AVP carried as was observed in a meeting where both groups participated).

During these meetings I said nothing. I either sat off to a side or at the table, partly depending on where I was told to sit. I did engage in conversations before meetings, during breaks, or after, but these conversations were mostly superficial since managers hesitated to talk in front of other managers (an important piece of data in itself!). As will be seen in Chapter IV, meetings were not the essential field for corporate activity, thus they provided an important but secondary source of data. I originally assumed meetings would be more central to management activities and had to change the focus after about two months of fieldwork in order to investigate the emerging patterns in the data.

Lastly, company documents were reviewed for data. Throughout the ethnography they play a minor, but at particular points, an important role. Company documents always kept to the formal, official view of the company and its personnel. Thus, other than for data on formal processes and the role formal processes play in the corporation, company publications were of limited value. The explanation of career development given in Chapter III, for example, would not be the explanation found in company hiring bulletins. The main relationships between the formal process as found in company publications and the more primary informal process is that once a rule had made it into the formal process it was very difficult to remove and thus had to be openly obeyed. For example, a vice-president publically permitted a certain manager to take over a function, and even though it was learned that this manager had misreported the facts to get the new function, the VP did not reverse his decision for fear of looking weak or indecisive. In this way informal factors were limited by formal ones. Hence, company publications were important in that they explained what the informal actions were responding to.

With these sources of data and the fieldwork techniques elaborated above and the theories and concepts discussed earlier in this chapter this ethnography was carried out. It had four phases: one, pre-fieldwork phase where a theory of culture was developed and a plan for application was devised; two, eight months of full-time fieldwork; three, four and a half months of analysis and categorization; four, five and a half months to write a first draft. Ethnography is about details: the finding, ordering, and presenting of the patterns of social life as they are found in the details of everyday experience. It is only in isolating what might be called the stylistic features, the marks of attitude that give it its peculiar stamp, that management will eventually be understood enough to know whether our general theories are general of anything that exists.

ENDNOTES

1. Rosabeth Moss Kanter. Men and Women of the Corporation (New York: Basic Books, 1977).

2. William H. Whyte. The Organization Man (New York: Simon and Schuster, 1956).

3. Talcott Parsons and Edward Shils. Toward a General Theory of Action (Cambridge, Mass., 1951).

4. Pitkin Sorokin. Social and Cultural Dynamics, 3 vols. (New York, 1937).

5. Ludwig Wittgenstein. Philosophical Investigations (New York: MacMillan Publishing Co., 1953).

6. Edward Shils. "Primordial, Personal, Sacred, and Civil Ties," British Journal of Sociology, vol. 8 (1957), pp. 130-45.

7. Clifford Geertz. "Suq: the bazaar economy in Sefrou," in Meaning and Order in Moroccan Society, by C. Geertz, H. Geertz, and Rabinow (Princeton: Princeton University Press, 1979).

8. Anthony F.C. Wallace. Culture and Personality (New York: Random House, 1961).

9. Interpretation is a universal process that human beings must use to think and to understand. Hans-Georg Gadamer. Philosophical Hermenuetics (Berkeley: University of California Press, 1976).

10. Clifford Geertz. Thick Description: "Toward an Interpretive Theory of Culture," in The Interpretation of Cultures (New York: Basic Books, 1973).

11. Ibid.

12. Louise Bernikow. "Alone: Yearning for Companionship in America," The New York Times Magazine, August 15, 1982.

13. Susan Sontag. "Writing Itself: On Roland Barthes," The New Yorker, April 26, 1982.

14. Martin Heidegger. "The Origin of the Work of Art," in Martin Heidegger: Basic Writings (New York: Harper and Row, 1977).

15. Philosophical Investigations.

16. Clifford Geertz. "The Impact of the Concept of Culture on the Concept of Man," in The Interpretation of Cultures, pg. 53.

17. Paul Ricoeur. "The Problem of Double Meaning as Hermeneutic Problem and as Semantic Problem," in The Conflict of Interpretations (Evanston: Northwestern University Press, 1974).

# Chapter II

## THE ECONOMICS OF MONOPOLY MANAGEMENT

### I. Introduction

The concept of economic structure is a subcategory of the concept of social structure. It enables us to collect and analyze cost and profit data which are an important part of any organization, since they effect the patterns of social action. Thus, it is appropriate to discuss, in a somewhat detailed manner, the economics of monopoly management. This will be done by: one, introducing the central principles of the theory of monopoly; two, describing the economic structures active in this utility; three, describing these structures in terms of monopoly theory; and four, interpret the meaning of uncertainty and the cost of information under conditions of monopoly management.

The economic foundations of monopoly management are fundamentally different than that of marketplace management. Since Adam Smith began the study of modern economics with his great work Wealth of Nations, the concept of monopoly and the concept of pure competition have been the two end points that define the field of economic theory. In the marketplace, price—the concept that determines when people will trade—is determined by long-run average cost of production.[1] This means that all the firms in an industry will lower their profits and increase their efficienty until profit is lowered to the point where less profit would result in the termination of production. This economic law is never realized, but its influence is pervasive in economic action. Thus, marketplace managers determine their supply positions by guessing

at marginal profit (profit made on the $n^{th}$ unit produced). This added
to the economic law that demand for any good is a negative function of
price means that in economic activity an "equilibrium" will be reached
where suppliers will make available x number of goods and demanders
will purchase these goods at y dollars per unit.

Nothing could be farther from the case under conditions of monopoly. Even though it is most certainly the case that monopoly managers
attempt to maximize utility as do marketplace managers, it is not the
case that they attempt to maximize profit.[2] Monopolies in the United
States always run the risk of legal intervention under the laws of the
Sherman Anti-Trust Act. Thus, monopolies must be careful not to be
seen by the public as making too much profit.[3] If they do, they
could be forced to sell off part of their assets as was done in the
oil and chemical industries earlier in this century. Hence, monopoly
managers would attempt to maximize utility by maximizing non-money
forms of income (e.g. company cars, extended vacations, increased
subordinates to lower workload). As the economist John R. Hicks has
said, "The best of all monopoly profits is a quiet life."[4]

II.  Description of Economic Structures

That a quiet life had been preferred at this utility is no doubt true. But before going on and specifying what exactly this "quiet life" amounted to, we need first describe the economic structures at place in this utility in order to take into account the particular structures and constraints that were on the minds of these monopoly managers. First let us look at the financial aspects. The most central financial constraint operating in this utility was that an earnings ceiling was set and specific prices were controlled by "tariffs." This meant that the utility would receive its income stream from the public, but the profit for each product would be legally set by state regulators. Thus, the most important concern of monopoly managers was gross cost. They concentrated on keeping cost below the estimated income level in order to maintain a "fair profit."

With emphasis on total cost, the utility manager looked toward productivity rather than profit. Profit was nonproblematic since they simply decided how much to spend, and since revenue was fairly predictable in a slow growth state, with stable technology and monopoly conditions of trade. They simply subtracted spending from revenue and got profits. And since this utility only asked for rate increases five times in the last fifty years and not at all between 1956 and 1971, we can be certain that profits had historically not been a problem.

The emphasis on productivity, then, and the emphasis on total cost, meant that there was not a need for an integrated budget which compared product lines, because only totals mattered. If there was a shortfall, then a project would have to be cutbacked, but this would not be done on a criteria of profitableness. It would be done on a criteria of most service to the community in general, and through the manipulation of information by self-interested, power-seeking managers. Hence, in the conceptual worlds of these managers there was a break between the concept of revenue and the concept of expense. Expense did not have to be financially profitable, but politically viable, thus there was no need to think of an expense in terms of total revenue. Only total expenses mattered, prioritizing expenses was not a financial problem, but externally a service problem and internally a political problem.

The reason the government agreed to such an arrangement was based on the idea of "averaged costs." This meant that the government decided that all the unit costs in the universe of total telephone costs should be averaged into one cost and that cost should be charged everyone. Thus some individuals would be subsidizing others (e.g., city customers would be subsidizing rural customers because of lower costs in the city due to economies of scale). Furthermore, there was another built-in tilt to this distribution system: business customers were in general charged higher rates over cost than were residential customers who were in general charged lower rates than cost. This was done by over-charging for long distance use, since most long distance calling was done by business. At this utility, five percent of the customers supplied fifty-five percent of the revenues.

Thus within the universe of local telephone use, the goal was to charge the least average cost, and further lowering of this price by cross-subsidizing through over-charging on long distance use. Over-

charging on long distance meant that these users were contributing
more than their numerical share to total revenue. This process was
monitored by a Federal Communications Commission (FCC) designed accounting system. The accounting system was applied on a national basis to
insure uniformity for all telephone charges in the United States.
This was clearly the act that caused local phone service to expand to
near universal use. Hence, the poor were able to gain access to phone
service for health and safety benefits.*

The most important method for the accounting system to finance the
average cost approach was the way it handled depreciation. The labor
that was used to put in a phone was not charged to expense as would be
the case in marketplace management, but instead was charged to capital.
Thus, phone bills were once again made to be priced under cost. Also,
this meant that the telephone industry would have a much larger capital
investment. Now the method used to depreciate this capital, so that
true cost would be deducted from revenue, was done by averaging. For
example, if two poles were put in, one lasted ten years and the other
twenty years, then much of the investment was not charged to costs
until the twenty years was up, since only then was the average life of
the two poles known. This put an emphasis on the long-run. And this
rate of depreciating, which was set by the FCC, was many times of a
twenty to thirty year period.

Because the telephone business was not able to get its capital
back quickly, it tended to not introduce new technology until much of

*A major theme of this corporate culture was that the managers were
protectors of the weak. They imagined themselves as serving "little
old ladies in tennis shoes." This point is elaborated in Chapter IV.

the depreciation from the old technology was recovered. This worked fine when technological development was slow, but was less efficient when, in the 1960s, the field of voice communication and the field of data processing merged, causing the fastest developing technological revolution in human history.

Anyway, even with all these procedures and methods to provide local phone service at less than cost, this utility did not have a capital problem. Capital over the last twenty years and probably longer had been a "bottomless pit" which enabled the managers to "overwhelm problems with resources." Therefore, what they lost in local service, they made up in long-distance service and other sources of income (e.g., the Yellow Pages). Also, this scheme worked because of the tremendous technological achievements made by the Bell Labs which propelled cost savings all through this century. The transistor and the semi-conductor being just two of the more recent and well-known examples.

Moving on in the description of the economic structure of this utility, production aspects of monopoly management is the next focus. As was just mentioned, research and development was done at the Bell Labs, thus this utility was occupied almost solely with implementation and maintenance. The central question of implementation was a question of risk: How fast should new technology be introduced? These managers wanted to maintain good service and control costs. Thus, the monopoly manager would, not having to fear losing demand, attempt to keep old technology in place in order to get the most productivity out of a particular technology to reap the benefits of decreasing costs. But a point would come when the old technology could not maintain the level of service that was desired or the cost in repairs outweighed the benefits of increasing savings from decreasing capital investment (capital investment is continuously shrinking because of depreciation, thus lowering opportunity costs because lower cost of operation meant that less alternative investments would be competitive).

Just the time and place to institute new technology is necessarily uncertain, because of the imperfect information concerning the productive life of the old technology, and because of the imperfect information concerning the efficiency, the durability, and the maintenance of the new technology. Hence, even if the monopoly manager had the option to delay the introduction of new technology, he still faced an uncertain decision universe impelling him to assign prior probabilities (i.e. risk) to the questions of productive life, durability, efficiency, and maintenance.

One thing the monopoly manager did not do was decide whether to introduce new technology on the basis of profits. This is true since he does not have the accounting system to provide him with net cost, but only gross cost, thus he is unable to tabulate the profitability (in terms of dollars) of the new technology. Also, since he is able to delay the introduction of new technology, he is inclined to leave the old technology in until net cost is more than the expected net cost of the new technology. This leads to investment decisions that have long-term payout, in the case of this utility, up to fifteen years. Since realized costs are kept low by capitalizing labor and since capital was produced by cross-subsidizing, an ability to make large investments with little short-term payout is maintained.

Thus monopoly managers on the production line grew to hate change, because they had some choice for the rate of change they desired, and of course they chose slow rates since this kept costs low by squeezing productivity out of capital investment. This is one reason why we will find managers encouraged to manage similar to their bosses: If there is slow change, why are new management styles needed? In fact, on the production line (a line where almost all AVPs and VPs had to make their reputation) if one failed it was because of incompetence, not lack of control, since control was not a big problem due to fixed demand, fixed supply, and fixed technology.

It was this type of a situation that was responsible for the development of the army of statistical categories that was used to judge productivity, known as the "green book" or the "green dragon" or the "bible." Measurement of productivity made sense because stable technology and protection from competition meant that the inputs to productivity were predictable, so the object was not what to do, but how much can be done. And productivity units per hour was a way to increase production in this stable environment by bringing in, of all things, competition. Internal competition between production organizations was what organized the industrial development of the telephone system in the United States.

And all this was done on a nationwide basis because the same technology and management practices were needed to insure compelementality of different telephone companies. Thus, a centralized staff was provided to insure physical and managerial connections at least cost between the companies. So, everthing being the same, the green dragon was able to breath its fire into every suborganization in every company and end up with comparable statistics. This meant that each telephone company would have its decision universe considerably reduced, since many decisions were made on the grounds of the universal form, not that of the particular company. One articulate VP explained it as: The McDonalds employee brings the french fries out of the cooker the same way in Houston as he does in Harlem.

But unlike the McDonalds employee, the telephone manager was able, at great cost, to keep large supplies of inventories on hand: There was no "Telephone King" or "Big Telephone" across the street forcing him to maintain minimum costs. To win the statistics game the monopoly manager had to win it in the green book, and winning it in the green book meant control. Large inventories were a way to increase control, to increase preparedness. Thus, production for these monopoly managers was not a matter of creativity or speed, but a matter of quantity of work (and quality as judged by categories like "courteousness" to the customer, which was also in the green book), which was had by controlling the factors or inputs of production. In the same way technology could be tested until the probabilities of expected performance were approaching certainty, the other major factor of production, labor, could also be continuously "tested" until expected behavior was predictable (i.e. conformity or else nonacceptance).

III. Integration of Monopoly Economics with Monopoly Management

With this admittedly inadequate description of the economic structures institutionalized in this company (a dissertation could be written
on depreciation or the green book alone), the next task can now be
approached: integrating the economics of monopoly organization with
the management of monopoly organization. To begin with, the division
of labor should be described, since it determines the possible field of
managerial activity. In his famous paper, "The Division of Labor is
Limited by the Extent of the Market," George J. Stigler[5] argued that
production functions will increasingly be taken over by the marketplace
as an industry develops in size. That is, a host of specialized functions will begin to be taken over by entrepreneurs as they find that
profits can be made through the efficiencies of specialization. Well,
in the telephone industry it was illegal for many functions to be done
by anyone except the telephone company. Therefore, the telephone
industry had to grow through vertical integration.[6] If the telephone
company wanted a new service, they had to provide it themselves.

In economic terms this resulted in decisions being made by production concerns (generally defined) rather than profit. Thus, we could
expect cost not to be a key factor in the extent of vertical integration;
that is, cost will not directly influence the designing of the division
of labor because only gross cost will influence only total allocation
of labor, not specific allocation. This added to the fact that monopolies will raise production costs (as a form of income) to keep financial
profits at a minimum,[7] meant that the division of labor in a monopoly,
the opposite of a competitive bureaucracy, would expand vertically as

it developed.

Thus, monopolies will be cost ineffective in terms of profits and will have functions performed internal to the organization that would not have been performed in competitive bureaucracies. Now, to fill all these functions in a monopoly, functions that were not necessarily created because they earned a profit, monopoly managers will choose individuals not to lower costs and maximize profits, but to maximize their general, non-financial utility. They will seek pleasure. It has been found that the form of pleasure that many times manifests itself is hiring managers with similar social backgrounds and tastes.[8] Monopolies are a home for racism and sexism. And, as will be shown, this is just what we found in this utility. It was found to the extent of being ingrained in the promotion practices of the company and the tastes of individuals. Economic structure and cultural tendency combined to produce patterns of social discrimination (at the same time they bragged about their company being based on "universal" service).

A second way monopoly managers maximized their non-financial utility was by reinvesting funds (funds that could not be taken out in profits) in ways that enhance the manager's status and comfort.[9] Within the company we found committees that were continued even though they were deemed instrumentally inadequate. The cost of running a committee is considerable (e.g. salaries of members). So even though this company had a reputation within the monopoly system as being "cost effective," we still have to question expenditures, since the monopoly manager's conceptualization of cost was gross production cost, not opportunity cost. That is, production units per hour rather than alternative investments was the guiding principle. Monopoly managers asked if it was effective in terms of how much it usually costs to do a task, not whether the task should be done at all.

Thus, managers were encouraged to do it efficiently, but they were not discouraged from doing things that were done for their own status rather than for the company's long-term prosperity because the mechanism to do this, profit, was absent. This is a main reason, as we will see, why so much of a political nature was found in intermanagerial relations. Since decisions did not have to be made by profit considerations, there was no way to order priorities (other than the ambiguous, thus insufficient principle of maximizing service to the customer). Similar to the university where the tenure system gives professors a monopoly on academic functions (e.g. teaching the religion of expression) there is no major incentive for professors to invest their resources in cost effective teaching methods, thus we find professors with poor ratings but full classrooms.

At this utility status was gained by controlling resources (both capital and labor). In the case of capital it was handled, as we have noted, by intense political infighting. However, there still was a considerable measure of giving all organizations an annual increase in funds. Thus, the political infighting was for the marginal dollar, or the dollar that demonstrated importance in terms of net dollar increase over previous budget distribution. Hence, the intense political infighting among the power centers was a cultural phenomena more than an economic one, since economically the advantage gained was an insignificant one. (Here we refer to culture as the culture of political motivation.)

Controlling labor was a bit different, since it was not only how many subordinates one had but who the subordinates were. As we will see, certain racial, sexual, and behavioral types were preferred. This discrimination was costly, since it lowered the supply of potential candidates.[10] Hence wages would be higher. Even though it was not possible to get conclusive data on wages, some suggestive information was obtained. A secretary said that a study found secretaries at this utility to be the highest paid secretaries in the city. A first level manager did not like her job, but said she could not find an equivalent job that paid thirty thousand dollars a year. A division head manager assured me that the utility pays higher salaries and gave as an example the fact that he earns more than his peers from his college graduating class that have equivalent jobs in other companies. A manager in human resources said that the utility did a survey of salary levels in other industries and found the utility to maintain the highest level of salary. In 1980 the AVPs were given a small wage increase and were told the reason was that they were already receiving higher wages than their counterparts in other industries. Thus racial and sexual purity, maintained by higher salaries, was a pillar of the "quiet life" in monopoly management.

From an economic point of view the tendency for managers to gain status by controlling large numbers of employees is a perversity, and it is a further perversity to pay higher prices for this labor not on the grounds of productivity, but on the grounds of racial, sexual, and behavioral criteria. This leads to the conclusion that what was important to these monopoly managers was social security and social appearance. Social security is a social relationship based on fears of alienation. The alienation comes about from noticing differences between oneself and others. If one fears there is something wrong with himself, he will react to differences in other people as evidence there is something wrong with himself. So he attempts to involve himself with others who are similar to himself, lowering the disturbing signals that provoke his fear of inferiority. Social appearance preferences are the cultural manifestation of this fear. If the fear pervades the whole group, then if becomes a status to express the remedy for the fear by insuring to all that can see that there is no reason to fear, since uniformity is under control. Culture plays an interdictory role in this regard.[11] It holds collective fears in suppression. The major theoretical point here is that since monopoly managers pay less for their actions (since opportunity costs are less due to protection from competition), non-economic cultural influences have more power to influence decision making because the cost to do so is economically less.

The only check on the economic cost of these cultural influences is the regulatory body. But these regulators and their staff will only be concerned with economic costs that are publically noticeable.[12] They will be concerned about public awareness and the costs and practices that could be easily learned by the public. And also the regulators do not have a standard for cost comparison, since a monopoly precludes this situation.[13] In fact, the regulators and managers will have many common interests, such as keeping the public content.

Of course these common interests are volatile because of journalists, social scientists, or because of, and this is probably the most important, ambitious regulators or managers. Nonetheless, regulators (working part-time in this case) do not have the interests or the abilities and resources to know the true costs of production.

## IV.  The Meaning of Uncertainty and the Cost of Information

We saw earlier that monopoly managers would hesitate on new investment of technology to insure maximum productivity (thus lowering the
cost) of old technology.  Monopoly managers avoided the risk of instal-
ling new technology until the old technology was demonstratively
inadequate and new technology was tested and retested until its operational efficiency could be predicted with accurate probabilities (historically speaking).  Furthermore, because of an upper limit on profit
and legal protection from competition, but no protection from losses
of overexpansion, monopoly managers will wait until demand is already
in existence before building new service structures.[14]  The regulators,
who are responsible for monitoring capital investment, and who are in
office usually as a stepping stone to higher levels of government,
have similar interests.  Overexpansion would make them look incompetent
and would have a damaging effect on their interests in attaining broader
governmental responsibilities.

So we see risk is kept as low as possible.[15]  Risk--a historically
developed ratio to predict outcomes in a certain class of action[16]--is
not, however, the only threat to control over outcome.  The more
pervasive threat, even in the telephone monopoly, is uncertainty.
Uncertainty is a situation where the variables are unclassifiable
because of their uniqueness; they do not demonstrate the common properties that are needed to classify them with past situations in which
the outcome is already known.[17]  These situations are the majority
of situations that are faced by all managers in all organizations.[18]

However, risk is related to uncertainty:  The more situations that can be classified in terms of risk, the less situations that are uncertain in a decision universe. Hence, the utility managers most certainly faced less uncertainty than their counterparts in competitive industries, since due to their option of waiting and seeking more data than a market manager was able to do, they could wait until the situation was classifiable in terms of past experience. In this way uncertainty was reduced, and risk--a known probability--was more often faced.

But time is a cost, since searching for information meant using resources that could be used for alternative investments.[19] The cost of searching for information is the profit that is foregone by passing up alternative investments. Hence, the level of uncertainty in the work world of a monopoly manager was a trade-off in favor of control (know-ledge) at the expense of marginal cost. In the case of utilities, management is geared toward a certain kind of problem: The problem of production.[20] The language system of mathematics (especially the sub-system of engineering) is the primary kind of symbol manipulation the utility manager is trained to perform. This is primarily a risk sort of decision universe. With fairly accurate data, the proven formulas of engineering can produce reliable probabilities. And as we saw, accurate data was secured despite the rising marginal cost.

The world of uncertainty is another world. Mathematics is useless; since the data is uncategorizable, it is not apparent in which formulas it might be used. The ability to deal with uncertainty is a gift of grace, it demands a creative spirit to invent new categories to bring the new observations down to the store of known experiences.[21] And these categories, because of their originality, cannot be proven a priori. Their imprecision, their ambiguity, forbids their manipulation in any sort of mathematical formula, since their identify is not operationalizable.

This sensitivity for guessing is weakly developed in the monopoly manager. He does not develop his mental capacities in this direction, since he has the option not to. Perfect knowledge is costly,[22] but protection from competition weakened the threat of higher costs for information search to the point where it could be considerably ignored by the monopoly manager. For the monopoly manager, uncertainty could usually be reduced to risk, since cost in the form of time (to collect information) was legally made very cheap by outlawing competition.

Shumpeter's principle of "creative destruction"[23] that propelled economic development from the feudal economic system through the various stages of capitalism, is not at work in a monopoly. As long as the monopoly can command its monopolistic integrity, it can control the rate of economic and technological development. The boom and bust that has characterized the history of capitalistic business cycles need not be so extreme in monopoly organization since many more variables are under control (however the level of economic development is generally lower).

It follows if uncertainty can usually be reduced to risk and if time becomes almost a free good, that the monopoly manager will construct his information collection process in order to be internally consistent rather than adaptable to a changing world. Even though there are limits to this non-adaptability because no monopoly is absolute due to higher probabilities of substitution as price increases.[24]

But regardless of this eventuality, there still exists a monopoly power that can demand that the world adapt to it, definitely in the short-run and within certain price limits this is true in the long-run.

Thus for the monopoly manager the meaning of supply and demand is not a continuing movement that demands managerial attention, but is a stable set of variables. In fact, it tends not to be a set of two variables that have to be matched, but is a single variable that is understood from the production function for the product. Hence, we should not be surprised to find the godhead "service" used by these utility managers to conceptualize a single action where under market conditions the term "service" would only cover a part of the actions needed to provide an adapting supply.

The conceptual world of the monopoly manager is simpler than that which is needed in the marketplace. In the marketplace the conditions of supply and demand, and therefore the distribution of asking prices, change over time.[25] In this situation the market manager must continuously search for information so that his product and its price will attract buyers. His conceptual abilities to carry out this search are one of his major capital investments and they are an irreversible investment.[26] And by its nature, once the investment for information collection is made, the ability to search is structured in such a way that searching in some directions is cheaper than searching in others.[27] But since supply and demand are continuously changing, and since the market manager must continuously change his price and usually his product to stay competitive, investment in new frameworks for search are also continuous. This is a high relative cost, since there are "set costs" in each framework that are not usable in new frameworks, thus continuous investment is necessary.[28] Furthermore, if costs of alternative search frameworks are not equal, then the knowledge of prior probabilities and utilities must be used in all cases.[29] Therefore, there are both cost as well as personal-structural reasons that the ability to search for information is scarce (i.e. costly).

Monopoly management, on the other hand, does not have to deal with this continuous rate of change. In fact, even during times of radical change in the environment the monopoly (if it remains a monopoly) can choose to not search out information to remain at that level of profit, but can cut back on profits and still survive. This is so because it would take a long-run adjustment in demand before substition could eliminate all monopoly profit. The monopoly manager hates change, because he is rewarded by production and production is maintained through control. Change is the opposite of control.

So we see that the monopoly manager does not feel inclined to continue to reinvest in new frameworks for searching out new information. This is so because new frameworks mean new information and new information means change and change lowers his ability to produce because of his inability to maintain continuous decreasing costs of information and continuous economies of scale in plant structure.

The heart of the matter is that for the monopolist the value of search in the face of price dispersion is absent.[30] The monopoly manager does not need the sophisticated search capabilities to stay competitive (not to mention that these search capabilities are primarily qualitative and irreducible to quantitative notation). Neither is the customer of monopoly products in need of search to find out if that product is up to competitive price and quality—this point is the flipside of the monopolist's search practices. Since the monopoly manager knows that his customer is not comparing his product to an alternative product (except in terms of substitution which are mostly irrelevant in the short-run and only commands attention in the long-run if new technology or considerable price increases come into the situation), he can come damn close to ignoring information about demand in day-to-day operations.

## IV. Conclusion

Therefore, the reduction of the complexity in the monopolist's decision universe leads to a primary focus on internal processes of the organization as opposed to market processes. In the conceptual world of the monopoly manager supply and demand complexities were reduced to "service" and service was fundamentally production. And production is a human affair, 'all too human'. The AVPs were a "club," the VPs had "forgotten how to work," if a manager "got the right number on his back he could move three levels," attitude was measured in terms of conformity, enthusiasm was channeled into control, and control was the backbone of power. In this "economic" organization, culture was paramount. The economics were simple, external politics a little more challenging, but the center of internal cooperation was a quagmire of constantly shifting, selfishly motivated, and informally implemented interaction.

ENDNOTES

1.  C.E. Ferguson and J.P. Gould, <u>Microeconomic Theory</u>. (Homewood, Illinois: Richard D. Irwin, Inc., 1975).

2.  Armen A. Alchian, "Competition, Monopoly and the Pursuit of Money," in <u>Economic Forces at Work</u>. (Indianapolis: Liberty Press, 1977).

3.  Aaron Director and Edward H. Levi, "Trade Reguation," <u>Northwestern Law Review</u>, 1956.

4.  John R. Hicks, "Annual Survey of Economic Theory: The Theory of Monopoly," <u>Econometrica</u>, January, 1935.

5.  George J. Stigler, "The Division of Labor is Limited by the Extent of the Market," <u>The Journal of Political Economy</u>, June, 1951.

6.  This is unlike General Motors which has had to increase vertical integration, because as it decreased in size, it was no longer able to support many businesses that specialized in one particular need. Thus, General Motors had to take over these functions in order to have them supplied at all.

7.  Alchian, op. cit.

8.  Gary S. Becker, <u>The Economics of Discrimination</u>. (Chigaco: University of Chicago Press, 1957).

9.  Alchian, op. cit.

10. ibid.

11. Philip Rieff, <u>The Triumph of the Therapeutic</u>. (New York: Harper and Row, Publishers, 1966).

12. Randall Bartlett, <u>Economic Foundations of Political Power</u>. (New York: The Free Press, 1973).

13. Alchian, op. cit.

14. ibid. This assumes that the monopoly is functioning at its profit limit. Alchian states that this is usually about six percent of revenues. If it is below this point, then monopoly managers will act similar to competitive managers and attempt to maximize profit. But once the monopoly manager reaches six percent, he will switch to nonpecuniary forms of utility.

15. In competitive industries entrepreneurial managers will seek out risk because this is their only means for growth in both sales and profits in the long-run. Because of their special talents for guessing at patterns where others see chaos, the entrepreneur is most at home in economically dangerous environments.

16. Frank H. Knight, Risk, Uncertainty, and Profit. (Chicago: University of Chicago Press, 1921).

17. ibid.

18. Jacob Marschak, "Economics of Inquiring, Communicating, Deciding," American Economic Review Papers and Proceedings, 58: 1-18, 1968.

19. George J. Stigler, "The Economics of Information," The Journal of Political Economy, June, 1961.

20. This is what happened with another American monopoly, or more precisely a member of an oligopoly, General Motors. A main reason for their recent demise is that because of their insulated economic functioning they concentrated too much on production rather than adaptability to market changes. The oil crisis happened and their market share was drastically reduced by Japanese automakers who were more alert and well rounded in terms of skills. And the important point here, is that not only is GM oligopolistic and not a monopoly, but it is only sixty percent, or so, the size of the telephone system in terms of both assets and employees! This should give some idea of the foreignness of market adaptability of the telephone company manager.

21. Knight, op. cit.

22. Marschak

23. Joseph A. Schumpeter, Capitalism, Socialism and Democracy. (New York: Harper and Row, Publishers, 1942).

24. A recent example of this is the OPEC oligopoly. As they continued to raise prices on oil, alternative products such as nuclear power and coal (and eventually solar power) became substitutable as supplies of energy. No good is infinitely inelastic. The telephone monopoly did not run into this problem too much, since prices remained stable or decreased because of tremendous technological innovation from the Bell Labs. The question can always be asked, however: Under competitive conditions would the price have fallen further? We could guess that the recent court decision means that some thought it could.

25. Stigler, "The Economics of Information."

26. Kenneth J. Arrow, The Limits of Organization. (New York: W.W. Norton and Company, 1974).

27. ibid.

28. Marschak

29. ibid.

30. Stigler, "The Economics of Information."

Chapter III

THE CULTURE OF CAREER DEVELOPMENT

I.   Introduction:  An Interview

So you want me to tell you why these fifty were promoted to the
top.  I'll be eighty years old this June and I've been retired for
fifteen years, so I don't know how much I can remember.  I started in
the telephone business in 1924, I worked for Bell for forty-three years.
I was considered one of the most outspoken vice-presidents of human
resources in the whole system, I had that job from 1950 to 1967.

When I came into the job managers were being held down because one
person didn't like them, we tried to break this up.  We set up a program
of continual appraisal, of group appraisal.  We started out by testing
them at the bottom of the hierarchy, but after this we believe in
appraisal, not only boss's appraisal, but boss's boss's appraisal.

Before the 1920's we had college recruiting; the recruiters would
go to State and make offers to all engineers.  They hired a lot of
people but none stayed around.  After World War II this changed and we
started choosing people on class standing, extra curricular activities,
and calibre of college.  AT&T knows more about colleges and recruiting
than anybody because we have been doing it longer.  We started recruiting
the best students at small colleges, no other businesses were doing it.
We had a policy that the people we hire into the college graduate
program should have the potential to hit at least third level; we gave
them special attention.  It started with a two year indoctrination
course.  They were given selected jobs and moved around through all the
departments.  Noncollege people were watched also, but college skills

61

helped move them ahead quicker in the early years of their careers. In the 1930s, 1940s, and 1950s, thirty percent of our best people did not go to college. We had vice-presidents and assistant vice-presidents without college diplomas.

I kept extensive records on each third level manager and up. I had a color code scheme where every third level and up was appraised by color, I kept this in my desk. By color he was rated as: one, could not go higher; two, could go one level higher; three, could go two levels higher. I personally, and my people, looked at college graduates to see how they were doing--are they progressing toward third level? If not, why not?

If a third level job opened up we would get together--the general operations managers (fifth level) from each geographic area, the senior operations vice president, and myself--and decide who gets the job. The chief executive officer (CEO) did not sit in these meetings but had a veto over any decision we made--he only overturned the group decision once in seventeen years.

One of the biggest issues during this period was training. I was very very strong on training. I learned that if I spent money on training I got results back that paid for the training many times over. After World War II we started nontechnical training. We were the only system company to validate this new training course. We set up a course, set objectives, got advice from academics. After people went through it, we checked up on them by questionnaires and interviews. We eventually started getting selective and sending people to specific programs if they showed potential.

I master-minded the Institute for Humanistic Studies at the University. A professor of industrial psychology advised us on this. We used him as an advisor during a bad strike we had in 1951, then set up the program the following year. We followed the careers of the Humanities graduates for ten years. The Institute was a big success. David Rockefeller liked it but could not sell it to the top executives at Chase. Three out of the four top people at AT&T today went there. If you had officer potential (sixth level), we sent you there. AT&T had programs at Williams, Dartmouth, and Swarthmore. We sent people to Wharton (it wasn't worth a damn), Columbia, Northwestern, and the Sloan Program at M.I.T. We tried to pick people who had the greatest potential to send to the programs. If you were coded blue on my chart that meant you had potential for two or more levels advancement. So if you were on the third level, this meant you could make it to fifth; you can't figure these things too far ahead, so we didn't appraise which third levels would make it to sixth level.

We had not hired anybody all through the depression and the war. The result was that in the 1950s all officers were within two years of each other's age and two were older. This was the toughest job I ever had to do--bring in younger men. This meant promoting younger people over older people who were better qualified. If you need five you had to pick fifteen because you knew some would not make it. This was one of the most distasteful things I ever did in my life. Some of the guys who are officers today moved quite fast to solve this problem---Lintz, Roberts, Platt. This was done at all levels. It meant heartaches all over the corporation. People were held back for three or four years because of this. I knew what this was like because I was third level in the traffic department [operator services] for eleven years because there was no career movement during the depression and war; we were cutting back a lot. This was a period in my life where I was held back and frustrated, it was the result of the business cycle.

Anyway, back to the people you're interested in; we adopted a policy that these guys who were moving fast had to stay at one job long enough that any of the curves they threw would come back to them. These young kids didn't like this. A guy had to stay in one job until he licked that job, and you don't lick a job in a year, it takes some time. By the way, the other side of this coin is that some people reach the top and stay in their job too long. I was in human resources too long; I told CEO Godfrey he had been on the job too long, not adding anything new.

Now, let's see where was I, I told you about selection, I talked about training, oh yes, movement. If you move someone up a level you usually moved him into staff. Staff got paid less than line. Then you moved him back to line. As he moved up again, then back to staff. Also, we moved people around the state if they had potential. Leach was moved much too often. It affected his children; yes, much too often. He was a real sharp young fella, everybody wanted him, good talker, knew his job, did it well. He would have made a good marketing man. He is suited well for the public relations job he has now.

I was in on Hill's promotion to the top office. He came up through commercial. Names have a bearing on these people getting ahead. Appearance makes a difference. He was a nice looking guy, makes a good impression, good talker.

The CEO before Hill, Mathews, was a perfect example of luck and age. He would not have gotten the job if he wasn't younger than the rest of us. Mathews was a bright guy though he was different than the CEO before him, Godfrey. Both had come up through commercial. Godfrey had a lot more experience. Godfrey was better liked but could get tough with you. Godfrey was the better boss because he let you run your own job, he didn't get involved in details. He never told me what to do and backed me up. You feel good when your boss backs you. Mathews did not do this, he was more inclined to get into details.

Mathews let his wife horn in on company affairs. She did not like some guy and it affected Mathew's judgment. I was always strong on the rule that you don't promote a guy because of his wife. There is no question that a good wife can help a man and a poor wife can hurt him. A wife could hurt a man by being obnoxious in public or at social events.

One last thing on this career stuff. Different companies will change as top men change. The stage of history the company is in determines what type of people it needs. When I came in the business top people were engineers and plant people because we had to build the network. Then after World War II top people came from commercial [customer relations] and traffic because we had a tremendous demand of phone service to fulfill. Now as we head into competition, marketing people are the most needed.

## II. An Approach to Career Development in American Bureaucracy

The career development in this Bell organization during the post World War II years, up to and including today, was as much a form of adaptation to one's superior's emotional needs and job standards as it was a development of one's own self-control and expressive capabilities. The most illuminating fact of the eight months of full time fieldwork in this management society was the degree of distance between the standards enacted during subordinate-superior interaction and the standards enacted during informal conversations with a trusted, or at least temporarily trusted because of similar interests, collaborator. In discussions with each other most everything was analyzed in relation to the current problem at hand, coalitions formed and reformed according to how a particular problem affected individual interests. In discussions with me most people were willing to be "objective" about old bosses or even potential future bosses but most people had little negative to say about current bosses. The temporal frame of reference was primarily on the present. Personal attachments were strongest when they were currently employed, especially if concentrated on task responsibility or political coalitions.

The managers in the center, the ones with jobs that were vital to the organization's success, were extremely careful of what they said, when they said it, how they acted, but at the same time the same strong ambition that enforced these strict codes of conduct and self-control also demanded recognition for their superior accomplishments and performance. And there was no better way of expressing one's superiority than by exposing the inferiority of other successful managers.

Thus a tension always existed within the motivation of the individual. His belief in the need for status (i.e., to be shown deference)
and his belief in the need for personal success and independence (i.e.,
individualism) were in conflict.[1]  No doubt status seeking was the
stronger motivation, since otherwise the individual would not have
joined a bureaucracy to begin with.  Hence, as we shall see, status is
the main descriptive category in the study of American bureaucracy, but
American individualism plays a strong role in defining the status
category.  Managers wanted to be shown deference, but they wanted to
be shown deference because they were seen as successful and independent
individuals.  Therefore, the key to understanding career development
in this American bureaucracy lies in the dynamic relationship of hard-
ened individualism, emphasis on self-worth (in the utilitarian sense)
and the need to be respected and honored by others, the need to be
shown deference.

The result of a strong sense of individualism is that interpersonal
relationships are based primarily on personal characteristics as opposed
to rules and regulations or tradition.  This Bell company is primarily
characterized by emotive bonds and political coalitions.  Authority is
embodied first in the individual and second in his office.  The office
carries authority, but when viewed in the context of the whole corporate
pattern of relationships, it becomes clear that the vital concerns
of the company are given to individuals who have worked their way into
the center group.  If the environment changes and a particular job
becomes more important when it was not important previously, the occu-
pant of that job will be replaced by an individual acceptable to the

ruling group. It is much more complex than "of course we want our best managers in the most important jobs" because "best managers" are ultimately defined by cultural standards; that is, the tasks of most, or large parts of all, jobs are to balance off competing interests. Hence, a "cooperative" manager means a manager who makes decisions that reflect the interests of the ruling powers (it is another issue what cooperation means horizontally, here we are talking about vertical cooperation because vertical relations are responsible for promotions and job movement).

Thus authority is embodied in the individual by his personal relationship to the ruling group. This leads us to the important conclusion that authority in this organization primarily took the form of a charismatic authority. Charismatic authority is an attribution of sacredness to the person. This differs from rational-legal authority which disperses the charisma throughout the hierarchy of roles and rules. Both authoritative systems ultimately rest on faith; but one has faith in the legitimacy of the individual, the other has faith in the legitimacy of the system of rules.

The American people are a charismatic people, our emphasis on individualism leads us to want heroes for leaders.[2] Our culture was formed around the individual's relation to God not to his social group, since most of the first settlers came for religious freedom.[3] Also, due to the continent's physical isolation there was no fear of attack, which would contribute to the forming of strong social ties.[4] We do not, fundamentally, run our government nor our large organizations by authority that adheres to the rules of bureaucracy, but by authority established on personal relationships.  Kennedy, Nixon and Carter were all anti-bureaucratic leaders, each one set up personally authorized counter-organizations to do the job that the established bureaucracies were designed to do.[5]  Reagan, of course, is also anti-bureaucratic as is reflected in his belief to destroy much of the bureaucracy altogether "to put decision making back in the hands of individuals who know best" (read individual as charismatic authority).

The traditional concept of charismatic authority, the belief by the charismatic and his followers in the special gifts the charismatic has for order creating leadership,[6] can be seen to be just part of an expanded concept of charisma.  Charismatic authority, here, will be the belief in the legitimacy of concentrated personal authority of any kind.[7]  Since authority has life altering power--promotions, demotions, organizational restucturing--it has a certain amount of charisma associated with it always.  What the subordinate responds to is not just the specific delaration of the incumbent of the role--as the definition of rational-legal authority would have it--nor the extraordinary personal qualities of the individual--as the psychologized definition of charismatic authority would have it--but the incumbent enveloped in the vague and powerful nimbus of the authority of the entire institution.[8]  The fire of a charismatic leader like Anwar Sadat does not die out after Sadat's passing, but a flame continues to burn as long as a concentration of authority exists that provides order.  Authority is the structuring element that gives order to any organization without which it could not exist as a collective body.  This moves the concept of charisma beyond the realm of psychology and makes it sociologically applicable to large scale organizations where a concentration of authority is essential for the planning and coordination of large group activities. Charisma becomes "dispersed" or "attentuated" in various amounts to individuals throughout the organizations' authoritative structure—its framework of offices. It is most strong where deference is seen as most properly expressed, which is where authority is most concentrated. Thus we speak of a "center."

Now, as was said, in the study of this organization, authority was most apparent in the ruling group of "key personnel." Thus the dispersion of charisma throughout this organization does not necessarily follow the formal hierarchy; that is, for example, a vice-president does not necessarily have more legitimate authority than an assistance vice-president, especially in specific situations where an assistant vice-president might get the backing of the CEO. The dispersion of charisma flowed out from the CEO developing into an informal power structure that ultimately made the vital decisions on vital issues. The formal structure was not grossly out of line with the informal structure, but they definitely were not synonomous. There were a number of job transfers during the period of fieldwork that in effect brought the two structures more into line with each other. None-the-less, the belief in personal authority meant that informal processes would be the primary field for managerial activity, since legal authority must be impersonal, and since modern American bureaucracy is too young to have developed authority based on long standing traditions.

Our focus, then, will be on the center and its relationships outward covering all the vital—serious in the sense of ultimate concern or importance to the organization—individuals, offices, and functions that embody the imputed charisma. Our task will be to identify and analyze the guiding principles that are used by members of this collectivity to advance their careers in terms of hierarchical rank. The institutional charisma will be dispersed according to general categories which mark certain behavioral styles as appropriate; we will want to map out these categories and their interrelationships. The culture of career development will express what kind of individuals and what kind of behavior the organization values highly as expressed by its promotion choices and practices.

In the following sections of this chapter the description of the career development process will be carried out. The next section will provide an overall view of the promotion process. Sections IV and V will then discuss the demographic characteristics of the top forty-eight managers who were promoted by this process. Section VI will be on training. Finally, sections VII and VIII will analyze the deference system from a career perspective describing the primary role of personal relationships and the dynamics of these relationships in the career process.

III. The Promotion Process

The promotion process was dominated by a concern with status pride and a tendency to strict conformity. These characteristics were expressed in personal sponsorship (charismatic authority) from the top and social adaptation from the bottom. The ambitious manager must be "hungry" because he must be willing to change his personal style and be energetic enough to apply himself not just to his tasks, but also to the social mores of his boss and through him to his boss's peers. He must be accepted socially.

At levels one and two there was little awareness of the socio-political nature of the middle and upper management. Level three seemed to be the turning point. Up until this time it was generally true that

> "If a manager does well with his indices he can move three levels; you get the right number on your back and get somebody impressed with you that you have some talent and you're on your way to district head."

The management hierarchy shaped up as follows:

| Hierarchy | Population by Level |
|---|---|
| CEO | 1 |
| Vice President | 10 |
| Assistant Vice President | 40 |
| Division | 120 |
| District | 400 |
| Second Level | 2000 |
| First Level | 7000 |

The competition started to increase significantly between third and fourth levels. One division head remarked,

> "Starting with division level, three criteria are

important for promotions: one, how you respond to
other people, two, your political abilities; and
three, being in the right place at the right time."

Before this political and social skills are secondary as one district

head reported:

"I never stood by the elevator to talk to so and so.
I was not career minded before I got to salary level
nine (upper second level); before this people looked
out for me more than I did for myself. You got to
get along personally, I didn't cause any problems
and I did a good job, but I was not really trying
to get promoted. I had just taken the job, temporarily I was thinking, because we needed some extra
money."

Once a manager made it to district head, however, the work world
started to look different. He had been successful, he had been rewarded
with promotions because "the company" thinks highly of his abilities.
Furthermore, now some AVP or VP has taken an interest in the manager
and he is one of "his people" in the sense that the superior picked
the manager to train him and promote him further. At this point it
becomes apparent that the manager has much to gain in the way of career
advancement from being extra helpful, attentive, and hard working.
Also, at this point, it is important to note that district level jobs
usually have many subordinates. Hence, the manager's responsibilities,
both real and perceived, have increased dramatically. Many AVPs reported either district or division head jobs as the point in their career
where their style of managing people was molded.

The managers all knew that "you need a strong supporter on one
level higher than the level you want to be promoted to." Thus, district managers started to share in the institutional charisma because
of the strong bond (the investment in them) with an AVP. A third

level stated, "I should be moving shortly because I've been at this job too long. You should have several jobs at each particular level before promotion; at least two or three assignments before going upwards." It is at this point that the career, the company, and the promotions start to become the central object in the lives of many managers. They work ten hour days, go to school at night a few days a week, and even some weekends are spent at work or doing company work at home. As one division head put it: "You have to marry the telephone company to get into the AVP club. Work becomes an end for these people not a means."

If work became an end it was not work in the sense of a craftsman plying his trade, but in the sense of a politician. The politician does have work to do; he must write laws, balance public finances, organize public works projects, etc.; but his most important job is to win votes, and he wins votes by creating information about his accomplishments and suppressing information about his failures. He wins votes by winning support and he wins support by impressing his constituents. The manager has a similar job. Occasionally an individual came along that was head and shoulders above his competitors and drew attention to himself from sheer superiority. Normally, however, many managers rose to the promotion potential group and the differences in their abilities was not apparent to a majority of superiors. Out of the one hundred and twenty current division heads, forty-three are considered promotable, fourteen are high potential. Hence, the decision of which one to choose for a promotion to the AVP level, barring a specific job need which is rare and only found in one or two individuals, "is usually a negotiation process among the [superiors] involved and is riddled with disagreement." Similar to the politician praising his accomplishments and condemning the accomplishments of his competitor, the bosses do the same with their choice for promotion and the choices of their peers.

The case for any particular manager rests on his reputation. One develops a reputation by exposure. A fast rising district head said,

> "I rose fast because of high exposure. I had high quality work but one can get by without this. I had high management exposure and therefore I was able to get support. I did a good job when I worked for the AVPs and the VPs, so I developed a good reputation."

What separates the winners from the losers in many cases is the chance, the chance to work with someone with authority.

The best way to get the chance is to be liked. The best way to be liked in the fifties and sixties was to be eager to please and sociable. For the most part, as reported by a personnel manager, "golf played the role as the social ground for business purposes." An AVP added, "CEO Hill [tenure 1970-1976] said that he could tell about a person by his golf game better than anything else." During the 1950s and 1960s, "the work orientation was not as strong as it is today." This is probably true since the telephone monopoly was not under attack in those days and change was placid compared with the mid-seventies and onward. There also were more fourth and fifth level managers in the 1960s, thus more people to do less work. Today's managers have more responsibility and golf has taken a lower level of importance. Also, the new CEO, being from California, plays tennis, not golf. It is interesting to note, however, a past CEO, who had been retired since 1970, mentioned that the current CEO "has recently taken up golf."

Nonetheless, the CEOs from 1960 to 1976, when the forty-eight managers were on the rise, were strong golf enthusiasts. The evidence for the importance of golf is that the two best golfers out of all one hundred and eighty managers on fourth, fifth and sixth level are vice-presidents. Out of the nine vice-presidents that are now in office and were hired after the war, these two were the first to be promoted into the AVP group. One of them did not even play golf, but mastered the game after coming to the company. Four of the ten vice-presidents still play golf on a weekly basis during the season. Golf still plays a role in the company. According to an AVP:

> "Most of the time golf is tied in with a quasi-business related issues; it's almost always business related. When Mumford goes out to Western area to look at something he plays golf afterwards with a couple AVPs, Benton and Krass."

In the office of one AVP, there were plaques on the wall with "Robert Jones Golf Championship" written on them. Robert Jones was his boss. Once when talking with a VP, he mentioned, "No one knew Bran and he almost won the Summit golf championship a few years ago." He acted like this was quite an incredible event that this AVP could be so talented at golf and not be a central figure in the upper management ranks.

A new member to the upper management ranks as an AVP in 1978 did not have much golf experience. Upon arriving in the company and noting the situation she, as reported by one of her peers, "started practicing on weekends and going to the driving range on week nights." During three day conferences it was customary for the third day to be reserved for golf. One division head told, "After the conference, those guys would come back and be in awe of Snyder. They would talk and talk about how he was amazing on the golf course." The golf course was the place where social acceptance could best be gotten.

Social acceptance was primary. This frustrated the few who were work oriented, but they had to adapt if they wanted promotions. One successful operations AVP stated, "There did not use to be an emphasis on performance, you just needed an OK evaluation from your boss." His organization was run with an emphasis on performance, he saw himself as one of a new breed. The old breed, the ones who started after the war and were promoted in the 1960s, however, had to have a broader social orientation, and golf was just the central activity of this orientation. A division head stated,

> "The guys belong, behind the scenes, to clubs and
> are really good at it. Sports continue to be a
> key. Makum, Bradford and other VPs and the western
> areas people love to talk sports."

A woman manager, one of a small minority, stated, "Many times meetings begin late because the men talk about sporting events for the first half hour. This effectively excludes the woman." Another female manager reported,

> "Some groups of men have their own language that
> makes you feel like you simply don't belong. When
> I was transferred to Wintham's organization, they
> used all sorts of hunting and cowboy analogies;
> or worse, one guy would say we shouldn't do that
> because it would be like pissing in the wind."

During the 1960s, only men were promoted to top levels even though total company employees were three to one in favor of women; and only a certain kind of man. "There was a perpetual adoption process going on," replied one black manager. "You used to have to wear a hat and wear a white shirt. It was most important that you made the right appearance," added an AVP.

There is no doubt that appearance was important. Beyond dress and deference signalling, "You had to look like an upper manager." A district head analyzed,

> "People not as bright, not as good performance
> results, but they have that air of confidence
> about them, they might not know a damn thing, but
> they act like they do. A psychologist at AT&T
> studied top executives. He found that their common
> trait was that they look confident, talk confident,
> and act confident. The AVP in human reources,
> here, told me the same things about two years ago."

It is difficult to describe, but in interviewing the AVPs and VPs there was a common style that many of them displayed. As they were answering my questions they would sort of lecture me, every five minutes or so they would say my name to repersonalize the interaction. It gave me the feeling of talking up to an authority.

In addition, an AVP reported, "You had to be reasonably literate, a good politician, in many cases competency is a low priority, and above all you needed a sponsor to get you above the mass." An AVP reminisced about his sponsor:

> "The most important thing to rise in this company
> is to have a mentor. My mentor was Murdock
> McClain. The instance I became his mentee I was
> first level, he was general plant manager (fifth
> level). I went over and started talking to him
> about his name. Something about this conversation
> got McClain liking me. He told my boss he was
> interested in my performance; he wanted to know
> about it if I did a good job. I followed him to
> central area--he must have asked for me. He was
> VPGM in central area and that's where I got pro-
> moted to fifth level. He was also in eastern
> area when I got promoted to third level in

eastern area.

Some top managers were better mentors than others. An AVP replied, "When I was a management trainee a guy at fourth level had a lot of people go on in the business. Three VPs and six AVPs that are up there today worked for him." The same is true today. At least a half dozen current top managers passed through the organization of one AVP. This AVP is the highest paid AVP in the company. Groups in power control the promotion process. And the groups in power are the ones that are performing the vital functions for the company's survival. An AVP remarked:

> "Shortly after I came in the CEO retired. A new
> CEO came in from the commercial department. These
> guys wore hats, glib, good front, not the smartest
> people, good public interfacers, they came from
> business schools. When this CEO came in these guys
> started to move. When the next CEO came in from
> the traffic department, these guys started to move.
> The two most important jobs after the CEO, opera-
> tions VP and human resources VP, were replaced by
> traffic people. Then in 1965 with another new CEO,
> commercial people started to move. Four VPs were
> promoted from the commercial department."

The context in which promotions must be understood, therefore, can best be described by three dimensions: one, sociability, ability to win your boss's support and through him other executive support, the most important means of doing so was on the golf course; two, appearance, in the sense of conforming to a standard accepted type (this type including racial, sexual, and behavioral criteria); three, centrality, relation to the ruling power. If a mentor had power and the mentee had conformed (adapted) to the acceptable type, then the mentor's efforts at getting his subordinate exposure to other powerholders would be the subordinate's start. If a manager was a good golfer or executives liked him for his sense of humor or subservient manner, or if a superior liked a subordinate because of the way the subordinate asked about his name, the subordinate's career was on the way up. There were "implicit rules against taking women and blacks as mentees." Thus, the "perpetual adoption process" or as one woman put it, "career cloning," resulted in caste management.

IV.  Group Demographics

We have seen that the promotion process was characterized by a development of a personal relationship between the superior and the subordinate.  In this way a subordinate could win support from a superior for a promotion.  This personal relationship was based on the subordinate possessing certain social qualities.  These social qualities belonged to racial, sexual, and behavioral categories.  In order to describe these categories we will begin with the demographic patterns found among the top forty-eight managers.

The policy of no hiring, except four that were hired in 1941 just before the war started, between 1930 and 1946 was one of the major determinants of the managerial pool that was used to promote managers to the AVP level and VP level for the post-war organization.  Every manager on the AVP level today was promoted to that level after 1960. Every manager on the VP level today was promoted to that level after 1962.

All, except for the four hired in 1941, of the forty-eight managers were hired after the war.  Nineteen were hired after 1945 and before 1950  seven more were hired between 1950 and 1953.  The telephone industry, similar to many American industries, was in a stage of growth after the war.  Telephone service was in demand to meet the needs of a booming population and a booming industrial sector.  Its product, telephone service, was not new, it was already over a half-century old, just more of it was needed.  Thus the telephone company had to continue doing what they had done before the war, but just more of it, and for this more managers, along with everything else, were needed.

(See Chart One, p. 83).

It is no surprise then, that almost all the managers were veterans of military service. Twenty-five of the twenty-six that were hired between 1945 and 1953 were veterans of the Second World War, the other manager was a veteran of the Korean war. Out of the forty-five managers that data is available for, forty-three were veterans of military service. The forty-three broke down by branch as follows: Army, twenty-one; Navy, fourteen; Air Force, seven; Marines, one (the CEO was the only Marine veteran, the last CEO had been a Marine also). (See Chart Two, pp. 84 & 85).

One of the two who was not a military veteran was a woman who was recently hired from outside the Bell system, the only manager who did not work her way up the organizational hierarchy. Also, the CEO and a vice-president had not worked they way up this organizational hierarchy, but did so in other Bell system companies.* Thus, forty-five out of the forty-eight had spent their entire occupational careers within this one organization.

## Chart One:  Year Started

| Year | AVPs | VPs |
|------|------|-----|
| 1941 | XXX | X |
| 1942 | | |
| 1943 | | |
| 1944 | | |
| 1945 | | X |
| 1946 | XX | X |
| 1947 | XXXXX | XXX |
| 1948 | XX | |
| 1949 | XXXXX | X |
| 1950 | X | |
| 1951 | XX | |
| 1952 | XXX | X |
| 1953 | | |
| 1954 | XXX | |
| 1955 | | X |
| 1956 | X | |
| 1957 | XX | |
| 1958 | X | |
| 1959 | | X |
| 1960 | X | |
| 1961 | X | |
| 1962 | | X |

Total = 43

Chart Two:  Military Service

Assistant Vice Presidents

| | Branch | Rank | Years Served |
|---|---|---|---|
| 1 | Army/Air Force | First Lt. | 11/11/42 – 12/27/45 |
| 2 | Criminal Investigation | Staff Sgt. | July '46 – July '48 |
| 3 | Army Ordnance | First Lt. | Nov. '60 – May '61 |
| 4 | Army Ordnance | Staff Sgt. | Mar. '43 – Jan. '46 |
| 5 | Army | Spec. 3rd Class | Oct. '54 – Oct. '56 |
| 6 | Navy | Lt. Commander | Jun. '44 – Jun. '46 |
| | | | May '51 – May '53 |
| 7 | Army Infantry & Signal | Corporal | Nov. '43 – Apr. '46 |
| 8 | Navy | Mate 2nd Class | Jan. '44 – Jun. '46 |
| 9 | Navy | Mate 1st Class | May '43 – Jan. '46 |
| 10 | Air Force | First Lt. | '59 – '61 |
| 11 | Army | First Lt. | Jul. 52 – Mar. '54 |
| 12 | Army/Coast Guard | Cadet | Aug. '43 – Jul. '44 |
| | | | Jul. '44 – Dec. '45 |
| 13 | | | |
| 14 | Army | First Sargeant | '42 – '46 |
| 15 | | | |
| 16 | Army | | '46 |
| 17 | Army | | Feb. '46 – Aug. '47 |
| 18 | Army | Tech. Sargeant | '43 – '45 |
| 19 | Air Force | Corporal | Jan. '43 – Feb. '47 |
| 20 | Army Air Force | Sergeant | Mar. '46 – Sep. '47 |
| 21 | Naval Reserve | Lieutenant | '41 – '58 |
| 22 | Navy | Seaman 1st Class | Jun. '44 – Jun. '46 |
| 23 | Air Force | Captain | Nov. '57 – Jun. '58 |
| | | Reserve | '57 – '65 |
| 24 | Navy | Student Pilot | '42 – '46 |
| 25 | Army | First Lt. | Jul. '50 – Jun. '52 |
| 26 | Navy | Lieutenant | Jul. '43 – Jul. '46 |
| 27 | Navy | Lt., Sr. Grade | '55 – '57 |
| 28 | Army | Master Sargeant | Aug. '44 – Sep. '46 |
| 29 | Navy | Lt., Jr. Grade | Jun. '51 – Jan. '55 |
| 30 | Army | Captain | May '42 – Feb. '46 |
| 31 | Navy | Second Class | Jun. '44 – Sep. '46 |
| 32 | Air Force | First Lt. | Jan. '55 – Jan. '58 |
| 33 | Army | Staff Sgt. | May '43 – Apr. '46 |
| 34 | Army | Sergeant | '42 – '46 |

Vice Presidents

| 1 | Navy | Second Class | Nov. '42 – Jun. '46 |
|---|---|---|---|
| 2 | Navy | Lt. (J.G.) | '43 – '46 |
| 3 | Air Force | First Lt. | '43 – '45 |
| 4 | Air Force | Captain (reserve) | '57 – '62 |
| | | (active) | Sep. '56 – Mar. '57 |
| 5 | Navy | Lt. Commander | |
| 6 | Army Air Force | Captain | Sep. '41 – Jan. '46 |
| 7 | Marines | Lieutenant | '48 – '52 |
| 8 | Air Corp. | Master Sergeant | Jul. '42 – Sep. '45 |
| 9 | Army | First Lt. | Sep. '51 – Jul. '53 |
| 10 | Army | PFC | '59 – '60 |
| 11 | Navy | Lieutenant | Jul. '43 – Jan. '46 |

We see that a number of characteristics of this group are consistent across the majority of the group: began careers during the same period, had military background, and had single company careers. At this point we can add another common characteristic of the managers on the AVP and VP levels: age. In Section I we learned that the hiring freeze between 1930 and 1946 had led to a serious management problem that forced top managers to pass over for promotion qualified long-time employees because the entire vice-president level was in the same age group and would be retiring within a few years of one another. In replacing the retirees the same mistake was made again; for the most part, they filled the posts of these VP retirees and retirees on the AVP level and newly created posts on these levels with managers that were all within a few years of each other's age.

During the period 1960 to 1974 there were a high number, more than thirty-nine, of promotions made to the AVP level. The reasons for this were twofold: one, replacement of retirees; and two, the organizational structure was redesigned in the first half of the 1960s, which resulted in a multi-functional division of labor with a decentralized staff structure as opposed to the late fifties and earlier, when a functional with decentralized staff structure was in place. In the early 1960s, the multi-function managerial responsibilities were lowered from the "vice-president general manager" to the AVP level in a job titled "general operations manager" (GOM). The result of this was that three AVP jobs were combined in the GOM job, thus losing two AVP jobs; but along with the GOM job three new AVP jobs were created: general marketing manager, general personnel manager, and general facilities manager.

Hence, there was a net increase of two new AVP level jobs created in this design; and this had to be multiplied by four for the four geographic areas, thus eight new AVP jobs were created.

Now, with these eight new jobs and with the jobs vacated by retirees, as was said, more than thirty-nine promotions to the AVP level were made between 1960 and 1974 (in the early 1970s another restructuring of the organization took place which centralized the staff, thus many job titles changed and possibly a few more AVP level jobs were created). The important point is that over a fourteen year period, thirty-nine AVP level jobs that data was available on were filled, in the majority, with managers that are now within a six year age difference of each other.

Out of the forty-eight AVPs and VPs comprising the top two levels of the organizational hierarchy twenty-nine were born between the years 1920 and 1932. In 1961 and 1962 the three AVPs who were promoted to that level and who still occupy their offices are now ages 59, 58, and 56 respectively; in 1970 and 1972, a decade later, three promotions to the AVP level were made and their ages are now 55, 56, and 53 respectively. Hence, even though ten years had passed the pool of qualified managers being considered for promotion was still the same pool that had been born in the mid-1920s and had come to work for the telephone company in the late 1940s and early 1950s.

The average age on the AVP level is fifty-two (December, 1979). This by itself is normal in relation to the whole Bell system which has an average age of fifty-one for all AVPs.[9] The abnormal feature of this AVP age distribution is that forty-one percent are between fifty-five and fifty-nine years old as opposed to a twenty-two percent average for the whole Bell system.[10]   (See Chart Three, p. 89)

Not only are forty percent between fifty-five and fifty-nine years old, but a few birthdays away are most of the others--seventy percent are over age fifty.[11]  Thus, between the years 1985 and 1995, if they do not retire earlier, which is the trend, thirty-two managers of the forty-six (two will retire before 1985), will be forced into retirement; twenty-five of the thirty-two will retire between 1986 and 1991. Therefore, this company will face a serious managerial problem in the form of inexperienced managers in the majority of leadership positions across the top two tiers of the management hierarchy.  When I mentioned this problem to a senior officer, he replied, "I don't care if the whole AVP level retires tomorrow, we have plenty of depth."  Such is not the case.  If we take a look at the next level down, the division head level, the level that must produce the replacements, we find the same problem.  Twenty-six percent of the division heads are over fifty-five and fifty-eight percent are over fifty.[12]  In an inhouse study of this problem, it was reported,

> "The realistic fourth level (division heads) can-
> didate pool for projected long term fifth level
> (AVPs) retirement vacancies, at about one for one,
> is not adequate to provide flexibility in the
> choice of candidates regarding skills, background
> and experience."[13]

This division head problem is also out of harmony with the rest of the Bell system which reports that twenty-one percent of all division heads are in the fifty to fifty-four age bracket as opposed to thirty-two percent for this organization.[14]  One of the reasons this Bell company is out of harmony with the Bell system is that it is a "slow

## Chart Three:  Birth Dates

| Year | AVPs | VPs |
|------|------|-----|
| 1918 |        | X  |
| 1919 |        | X  |
| 1920 | XX     |    |
| 1921 | X      | X  |
| 1922 | XX     |    |
| 1923 | XX     | X  |
| 1924 | XXXXXX | XX |
| 1925 | XXXXX  | X  |
| 1926 | XXXX   |    |
| 1927 |        |    |
| 1928 | XX     |    |
| 1929 |        | XX |
| 1930 | XX     |    |
| 1931 | XX     |    |
| 1932 | X      |    |
| 1933 |        |    |
| 1934 | X      | X  |
| 1935 |        |    |
| 1936 |        |    |
| 1937 | X      | X  |
| 1938 | X      |    |

Total = 43

growth state." Fewer people moved into the state and fewer moved out. Not much turnover in the state was paralleled by not much employee turnover in the company. This factor amplified the age clustering problem. Since once hired almost all employees stayed at the company, and since there was not as much growth as other states witnessed, thus the needs for new personnel were less than in most other Bell companies. This factor, however, cannot account for the twenty-nine promotions to the AVP and VP levels between 1965 and 1976, since this issue of longevity has nothing to do with new promotion choices, but only with the lack of them.

The explanation for this age clustering phenomena is threefold. First, as was just noted, employee turnover was below average nationwide. Second, as we were told in Section One, most hiring took place after the war, thus the available pool for pomotions in the early sixties when the previous generation of clustered aged managers retired was filled with clustered aged World War II veterans. Hence the sixteen promotions to the AVP level, of the managers still in office, made during the years 1960 to 1965 (one of the sixteen was made in 1957), during the tenure of CEO Godfrey would have to be made from the postwar hirees, since the 1930 to 1945 period was hireless. These were the beginning of the "young fellas" that had to be rushed past their superiors to provide a semblance of continuity to management successions. The average age of these sixteen promotions in 1981 was fifty-eight years old.

The promotion process during this period was conducted by the human resources vice-president and the higher ranking operations senior vice-president. The CEO during this time, whose tenure in office ran from 1949 to 1965, functioned predominantly, as is traditional in the Bell system, as an interface with the community, thus not primarily facing internal matters. Hence, the senior vice-president ran the company. He also, it turned out, became the next CEO, but he, differing from the one who came before him and the two after, was a CEO predominantly concerned with internal matters.

He became CEO in 1965 and promoted thirteen managers to the AVP level, of the managers still in office, between the years 1965 and 1970. The average age of this group in 1981 was fifty-six years old. It is now the second half of the decade, but the average age of promotees to the AVP level is only two years younger. This CEO also had to promote six AVPs to the VP level between the years 1965 and 1969 because of the age clustering in the previous generation. The ages of five of the six VPs which data was available for are 57, 60, 56, 62 and 61 in 1981; all within five years of each other's age. Thus, simultaneously, top management is dealing with the problems of a clustered aged retirement group and building another clustered aged management group.

The next CEO came in, CEO Hill, and ten AVPs were promoted during his tenure, 1970 to 1976. The average age of this group was fifty years old in 1981. Even though it was ten to fifteen years past (see Chart Four, p. 93) the 1960 to 1965 problem of filling AVP positions because of mass retirement within this period, the promotees were still characterized in the majority, by being born in the 1931 and before group. There are no young highly talented managers in this group. It took an average of eighteen years (see Chart Five, p. 94) to become an AVP.

Thirty-eight of forty-two became AVPs between fourteen and twenty-one years. One had to go through the process, and the process was, as we shall see, not primarily a test of management skills. It is interesting to note that the only AVP to make it in thirteen years, who is generally "put up with by his peers" and has one of those careers that lately has been marked by miscellaneous assignments, was the son of a CEO of another Bell system company.

The third reason for this age clustering phenomena, since the first reason—low employee turnover rates—and the second reason—the hiring freeze between 1930 to 1945—could not account for the homogeneous age distribution characterizing the promotions made to the AVP level between 1965 and 1974, is that promotions were, in general, primarily based on criteria of social qualities as opposed to merit. That there is only one woman on the top two tiers, and she something of a token (see below) in a company that historically employed more females than males, one Jew, one of eastern european ancestry, no blacks, no orientals, no Italians, no Hispanics, not as we have seen, even too many younger men, begs looking into. And that is what we will do in the remainder of this chapter.

Chart Four:  Year Became AVP

| | Year Made AVP | Year VPs became AVPs |
|---|---|---|
| 1957 | | X |
| 1958 | | X |
| 1959 | | |
| 1960 | | X |
| 1961 | XX | |
| 1962 | X | XXX |
| 1963 | XXX | |
| 1964 | XX | X |
| 1965 | XX | XX |
| 1966 | XXXXX | |
| 1967 | X | |
| 1968 | XXXX | |
| 1969 | X | |
| 1970 | X | |
| 1971 | XX | |
| 1972 | XX | |
| 1973 | XX | |
| 1974 | XX | X |
| 1975 | | |
| 1976 | X | |
| 1977 | | X |
| 1978 | | |
| 1979 | XX | |

## Chart Five:  Years to Become AVP and VP

| Number of Years | AVPs | VPs Became AVP | VP |
|---|---|---|---|
| 13 | X | | |
| 14 | XXX | XX | |
| 15 | XXX | X | |
| 16 | XXXX | X | |
| 17 | XXXX | XX | |
| 18 | XXXXX | XX | X |
| 19 | XXXXX | | |
| 20 | XXXX | X | XX |
| 21 | XX | | XX |
| 22 | X | | X |
| 23 | | X | XXX |
| 24 | | | |
| 25 | | | X |
| 26 | | | |
| 27 | X | | |

V.  Group Demographics Continued

In describing the managers that occupy the central positions of
authority in this telephone company, we saw that they had many similar-
ities: started their careers in the period after the Second World War,
stayed in a single organization throughout their careers, were all
close to the same age, almost all were military veterans, and that
their ethnic background and sex were not characteristic of the broader
population.  As we continue the description of these managers their
characteristics will become more and more homogeneous lending support
to the proposition that social features of the manager were prime determinants in selection for positions of authority, since the common
characteristics shared across the group will be the characteristics
that are valued by the group, and since these individuals were chosen
from a broader, more socially diverse population.

In this telephone company, sixteen out of twenty-one that data was
available for in the group of forty-eight AVPs and VPs, stated that at
least one parent was of German descent.  Six out of the twenty-one
noted at least one parent of Irish descent.  Seven out of seven of the
VPs that data was available for show at least one parent of German
descent, one other VP shows at least one parent of Irish descent, and
for the two others data was not obtained.  Three out of three of the
VPs that were asked about both parents reported both parents of German
descent.

Out of the sixteen managers that were asked about religious up-
bringing nine reported Protestant and seven reported Catholic.  As was
mentioned earlier, there was one Jew in the forty-eight.  I would

guess that the remainder of the forty-seven were either Catholic or Protestant similar to the sixteen I have data for. It was not uncommon for remarks about church activities and attendance to be made at lower level management meetings. If a manager was an atheist or agnostic I would also guess that he would keep it to himself, since such things as divorce and alcoholic beverages were looked down upon at the telephone company. On the whole, social behavior was expected to be conformative in tone and conservative in temper. As one AVP said,

> "I never tell my subordinates I don't like beards
> or nonwhite shirts, but I tell 'em they never see
> me with a beard or a nonwhite shirt; I can't tell
> 'em how to dress, I just tell 'em that I don't wear
> these things, some people understand and some
> don't."

Most of the forty-eight managers were born and raised in cities and towns in the same geographic area as the company. Twenty-three out of the thirty-three AVPs that data was available for were from this geographic area; four more were from the neighboring state, two others from another neighboring state. Only four out of the ten VPs, however, were from the same state as the company. Partial explanation for this difference is that two VPs were transferred in from other companies in the system. Thus, twenty-seven out of the forty-four that data was available for are from the same state. Seven of these twenty-seven were from the state's largest city and seven others were from the state's second largest city.

All the managers hired after the Second World War that made it to the AVP or VP level started with a college education. Eighteen of the forty-four that data was available for had a bachelors degree in engineering. Although eighteen came in with engineering degrees there are

only four specifically engineering jobs on the AVP level and one on
the VP level. It was generally agreed that the five individuals that
won these positions were top qualified engineers. The other thirteen
engineering graduates developed skills in other management areas where
an engineering background was relevant but not primary. One out of
the five occupying an engineer's position had a degree in business
administration, however, he had been one of the ones hired in 1941
and when he was promoted to the AVP engineering job in 1966, he already
had twenty-five years of experience, nine in engineering and sixteen
in operations.*

Twenty-six out of the forty-four received their degrees from
colleges in the same state as the company they spent their lives working
for. Five degrees were from the largest state college, three from the

---

* It has been noted in other telephone companies that engineers have
a higher amount of "worldly naivete" than other management personnel.
[John Mills, The Engineer in Society (New York: D. Van Nostrand Co.,
Inc., 1946.] With certain qualifications this generalization finds
support in this telephone company. As a group, except, interestingly
enough, the one with the business education, the engineers were generally considered to be bright but apolitical. The vice-president of engineering was said "not to have a political bone in his body." Even though
his position was powerful in most other Bell companies he, with his fas-
cination with technology, was not a powerful figure in this company as a
whole or among his peers on the vice-president level. The AVP engineers
had some clout to stop projects other departments proposed, but many
times these individuals complained about the irrational fights over
territory that entered into decision making on both AVP and VP levels.
It was observed that in general this group of engineers were somewhat
frustrated from not being in the center of authority and more or less
just being used by powerful managers for their technical expertise.
They made a significant, some would say very significant, contribution
to the running of the company, but they were not directly involved in
the ultimate centers of power. One of the engineers was especially
frustrated because he faced an especially strong operations AVP in his
area and it was a generally acknowledged fact that his motivation and
commitment had suffered seriously from this. This was generally true
of this group if not to such a degree.

second largest state college, four from the state's largest private college, a group of three and a group of two from two medium sized private colleges, three from a small private college,* and the other six scattered about the state. (See Chart Six, pp. 100 and 101.)

After considering these patterns, first German, and second, Irish descent as the most numerous nationalities present; Protestant first and Catholic second as the two most numerous religious backgrounds; the majority born within the same geographic area by state, the same state as the company; all were college graduates (even the three managers hired in 1941 without degrees got their degrees at nightschool) with the majority attending colleges within the state, eighteen had degrees in engineering—and the previously mentioned demographic patterns—

---

* An interesting pattern worth noting is that two of the vice-presidents graduated from Patriot College. Patriot is a small private college, presently about two thousand students, in the 1940s it probably had less. CEO Mathews, discussed earlier, and before CEO he was Senior Vice-President, was also a graduate of Patriot. He was the individual of highest authority who took a careful interest in promotions to the AVP and VP levels throughout the 1960s. He not only shared this alumnus with two VPs, but had hired both of them. He hired one in 1941 and the other in 1947; two other people that he hired, one in 1946, the other I do not know, also became vice-presidents in the 1960s. Another Patriot graduate who is now an AVP and is rated VP potential is currently one of the three AVPs that will be "moved through" when the next VP positions become available. CEO Mathews, when I interviewed him at his home—he retired in 1970—said that this particular AVP, along with his daughter were rated the two most likely to succeed at Patriot in their graduating year, 1960. Also, Vice-president Stone, a Patriot graduate of 1940, said that this AVP was recommended to him by several professors at Patriot when he was there for a board meeting (both CEO Mathews and Vice-president Stone were on the board at Patriot). During discussions with Stone and Mathews, both took credit for hiring the now AVP (this is a recurring theme at Bell: whenever anything good happens, several different people take credit, see Section VII). The point here, however, is that a strong mentoring system exists, completely informal (one middle manager stated that the AVP from Patriot never mentioned Stone or Mathews in the five years he worked for the AVP). The dynamics of the mentoring system are played out in a context of deference. This is discussed in detail in Sections VII and VIII.

started career after the war, single occupation career, similar ages, and all were military veterans—it can be concluded that the managers responsible for promotions in the 1950s, 1960s, and 1970s were looking for a particular type of individual. But, as we will see, these were only the a priori patterns that had to be met, the others began where these left off. They were patterns for acceptable behavior.

Chart Six:   College Education

AVPs

| Number | Degree | Second Degree Later in Career |
|--------|--------|-------------------------------|
| 1 | BS Mechanical Engineering | |
| 2 | BS Economics | |
| 3 | AB Business Administration | |
| 4 | BS Accounting | |
| 5 | BS | |
| 6 | BS Electrical Engineering | |
| 7 | BS Electrical Engineering | |
| 8 | BS Electrical Engineering | |
| 9 | BS Electrical Engineering | |
| 10 | BS Mechanical Engineering | |
| 11 | BS | MS, M.I.T. |
| 12 | BS Electrical Engineering | |
| 13 | | |
| 14 | BA | Ph.D. Johns Hopkins, Economics* |
| 15 | | |
| 16 | BA Business Administration | |
| 17 | BA, BS | MS, Industrial Management, M.I.T. |
| 18 | BS Industrial Engineering | |
| 19 | BS Electrical Engineering | |
| 20 | SB Government | |
| 21 | BA | |
| 22 | BS Business Administration | |
| 23 | BS Business Administration | |
| 24 | AB English | MS, M.I.T. |
| 25 | BS Mechanical Engineering | MS, M.I.T. |
| 26 | AB Business Administration | |
| 27 | BS Electrical Engineering | |
| 28 | AB, MA | |
| 29 | BS Electrical Engineering | |
| 30 | BS Electrical Engineering | MBA, M.I.T. |
| 31 | BS Civil Engineering | |
| 32 | BS Electrical Engineering | |

*This belonged to the female Treasurer hired specifically to be a female treasurer in the all male management system that was ordered under a federal decent decree to integrate more females and blacks into upper management ranks.

| Number | Degree | Second Degree Later in Career |
|---|---|---|
| 1 | BS Economics | |
| 2 | AB Business Administration | |
| 3 | BA Business Administration | |
| 4 | BS Electrical Engineering | MS, M.I.T. |
| 5 | BS | |
| 6 | AB Engineering | |
| 7 | BS Industrial Management | |
| 8 | BA | |
| 9 | BS Electrical Engineering | |
| 10 | BS Industrial Engineering | MBA |
| 11 | AB History | |
| | MA Educational Psychology | |
| 12 | BA | |

VI. <u>Training</u>

The people who came to work for Bell after the war were, above all, choosing a company that provided first a secure and second a comfortable place to work. Bell did not lay off any workers during the depression; nor, and it was one of the less than handful to accomplish this, did it miss a dividend during the depression or war. It was common knowledge in America that Bell Telephone occupation was almost synonomous with security. At this Bell company, since the war, only one time were there layoffs, and then nonmanagement. It was in 1957, two hundred and thirty craft employees were layed off, but most were rehired the next year.

By choosing an industry that had no competition, by choosing a utility, people that came to Bell were making a safe occupational investment. By choosing an industry without competitors they were eliminating the strongest determinant of uncertainty in their work environment. The telephone industry still had uncertainty, but the years after the war were characteried by steady growth rather than audacious innovations from competitors stealing parts of their market share. In the telephone industry, if the telephone company did not do it, it did not get done!

The college trainees coming into the company after the war were taken to meet the CEO. Several managers recalled that the CEOs in those days used to tell the new recruits two things about the telephone company: "one, you won't get rich at the telephone company; two, what you learn here will not be transferrable to another industry." Hence, the new managers were emphasizing security over risk and profit and were starting out on a single occupation career.

Single occupation, however, was not so single at the telephone company. When asked why they came to work for Bell, many AVPs and VPs responded that it was because of the "general manager idea." This idea promised incoming managers that they would be moved around having a chance to try their hand at a multiple number of tasks. This was appealing compared to the engineering type job that was the only alternative at most other large corporations. Here engineers could obtain jobs in operations, most of them did, and manage large numbers of employees.

The usual training for these recruits was general supervisory training. They began with a somewhat emotion laden, it still is, introductory program stressing dedication and loyalty to the company and service to the community. Recently the drop out rate of the management development program is between sixty and seventy percent. What it was after the war I do not know, but it was probably less judging by the concensus that "dedication to service is not what it used to be."

Bell managers, then, started out being trained to supervise, not to come up with or sell new ideas. They got promoted for being good administrators. They were trained within functional boundaries and rewarded by the statistical results they achieved within those boundaries. They, of course, had to get cooperation across their boundaries to complete their jobs, but this was the informal system and not officially considered. Also, since they were public servants, and since they had a common interest only to serve the public, open conflict was taboo, so was aggressive marketing of oneself; conformity, consistency, and loyalty were the norms. "Surprises were considered a sign of disloyalty," said an AVP. Another AVP added, "Some of the CEOs and VPs would consider you the problem if you brought them a problem." Bell managers were encouraged to supervise smoothly, problems should be contained. Disturbance was bad.

Even without external competitors to worry about, the Bell manager, especially in the earlier years when technology was less reliable, faced a serious external threat: the weather. For example, when Hurricane Hazel hit in 1954, telephone service went out in a large part of the state. There were meetings at night to set up crews, around the clock shifts, intense efforts were made to get service back in operation. In many ways this was when the telephone managers were at their best, all cooperating to deal with an engineering kind of problem that attacked them right at their corporate heart: the public's ability to make phone calls. Operators were kept at their stations until flood waters receded and other shifts could get to work; meanwhile food and blankets were brought in by boat. One VP said that as a district head during a flood, CEO Godfrey pulled up in front of his office in a small boat with another man working an outboard motor on the back of the boat and asked if he needed anything; being a competent young district head manager he had already secured blankets and sandwiches for "his people." The way these crises were handled could have a lot to do with making a reputation for yourself and thus for your chances for promotion.

Once one "got [his] head up," usually this started at a low level, it meant someone up above was watching. As one district head third

level) said, "You can tell how well a person is doing by his job assignments, who his bosses have been and are, and the speed of his advancement." Thus the 'ones' that meet the  riteria are brought into the
center, they're given jobs of importance, jo s whose results are contri-
butions to concerns that are deemed vital by the higher powers. As one
division head (fourth level) stated, "If someone has miscellaneous
assignments over a long period you can assume that the person is not
valued by the corporation; they have little clout or power, side-lined,
not mainstream." It is important to note here that "the corporation"
is synonomous with individuals with authority. This same manager at
another time said,

> "If a manager is hot, that is, in trouble with the
> officers (vice-presidents) or the AVPs, or with
> just one important AVP or VP, then it is not
> advisable to be seen with them; and if they are
> your friend or you need something from them, it is
> best to call or meet outside the company for lunch."

In the case of the forty-eight AVPs and VPs, the most held position,
and a position deemed important because of its direct connection with
telephone service, was the division operations manager. Twenty-nine of
forty-four that data was available for held this job. Seven out of the
ten VPs held this job; five out of the ten VPs held the general operations manager job which is an equivalent job but one level higher.
Division operations managers were in charge of the "field troops" who
put in the equipment and maintained the central telephone plant (e.g.,
switching stations). These jobs were the heart of the Bell system;
they were measured quantitatively with hundreds of different service
measurements. Volumes would be published monthly that recorded, down
to the lowest levels, the comparative statistics of all Bell systems

operations and thus the managers responsible for those operations. In
this job you were on call twenty-four hours a day, day in and day out.
It was a front lines kind of job, directly responsible for telephone
service. It used to be that all general operations managers received
higher pay than other AVPs. It is still the case that operations and
engineering are higher paid than other AVP positions. The highest
paid AVP in the company is a general operations manager. In 1981
there were thirty-seven AVPs, five of these were general operations
managers. In 1981 six out of the thirty-seven AVPs received "merit
money." Four of these six were general operations managers. Until
the last decade service was everything, and it still is the majority
of everything.

So, if you were seen going through these positions it was generally
known that you were on the fast track. One VP told me that a Bell
company CEO should be on his way by age thirty-five. This early
potential marking had been a problem at one time according to an AVP.
He said,

> "Once they were marked that way the marking itself
> sometimes was enough to insure promotion, so we
> made it policy that you can only rate one or two
> levels ahead and that the boss's boss should also
> evaluate the manager."

This increased another problem, though:

> "When you needed someone you would want to get
> managers with two level potential instead of one;
> this really was unfair because different managers
> used different standards so that one guy rated
> two level promotion potential by one manager was
> preferred by some other manager using different
> standards; when in reality the second guy was
> better than the first. So who rated you became
> more important than what you were rated."

One other way besides job positions and speed of advancement that was a signal that the individual was considered high potential was training. As can be recalled from Section I, the Institute for Humanistic Studies was set up for this purpose. Five out of the ten VPs and nine of the AVPs attended the Institute in the 1950s. Also, five managers on the AVP level and one on the VP level were sent to M.I.T. to get graduate degrees in business related subjects. During the field work, several key division level managers were sent to executive programs for five week courses at various colleges. Just about all the AVPs had various plaques on their walls showing completion of one of these courses.

Also, during a third level position, managers were sent to AT&T for two years. The interesting point about these training programs and the AT&T experience is that most third and fourth level managers reported, it was close to unanimous, that these managers were simply getting their "ticket punched." They had already been picked for promotion and these programs, even the evaluative ones, were a mere ritual experience before continuing to the next level. Only the "favorite sons" went to these programs.

VII. <u>Subordinates Adaptation to Superiors</u>

As was said in Section II, the outstanding characteristic of career development in this management hierarchy is the deference system. Added to this we saw that an unusually high degree of conformity existed on the top two levels of the hierarchy. Now, we are ready to examine in detail the subordinate's view of the deference system in order to arrive at an understanding of how individuals perceived the funneled path to central positions of authority.

> "The most important career contingency at Bell is your relationship with your boss. You have to find out what he is like, what he needs and give it to him, so that he is supportive of you. You also have to do a good job at your work, no problems,"

described a division head. If you have a falling out with your boss, you're not dead, you're down. It was observed that a number of managers got promotions that years earlier had been on the fast track and then had a fight with their boss which resulted in a slow down of their advancement. They were put on the side until they got a transfer and gained support under another boss. The company was large enough that one could have an enemy and survive, but one could not have two.

One of the very few managers that worked in another corporation, a bank--organizations not exactly known for their looseness--said, "The CEO is powerful in a military sense, people see him this way. People respond to him this way, Bell people respond to position." Deference was given because it was perceived that it was expected. One fourth level manager was talking about another fourth level manager, "Boyd is a comer, he is the perfect example of a guy who is doing things that have to be done to get into the club." The "club" is the AVP level (see Chapter IV).  I had the good luck to be invited out to have drinks by a vice-president who was meeting Boyd and another fourth level manager after work.  Here's an excerpt from my diary of that meeting:

> "Boyd played up to Latant like he was Latant's
> girlfriend.  At one point he grabbed Latant's hand
> and started making feminine facial expressions and
> saying in a romantic voice things about later in
> the evening.  Latant stared between myself and the
> other manager with a bemused halfsmile on his face."

This event was in July, five months later Boyd was transferred into a central position in Latant's organization.

During the interview before we went out for drinks I asked Latant what he thought of another vice-president who had a reputation for having a systematic strategy for career advancement which consisted of "joining the same church and the same golf club of his superior when he was transferred to a new town."  Latant replied, "that's corporate survival."  In fact during the drinks Latant mentioned about an old boss, "Yah, he's something else, I saw him the other day and he mentioned something about the books; [looking at me], the books were the ones I used to help teach his daughter how to read."

An astute manager would win his boss's favor by giving him what he wanted.  Of course "you had to do a good job and have no problems" but this was not enough to get strong backing, backing where the boss would fight for his subordinate's promotion, and this is what he had to do since other bosses had other subordinates they wanted to promote.  More candidates than openings meant conflict.  Hence an ambitious manager would try to build a strong emotional tie between himself and his boss in order to get the boss personally involved in the manager's life.  One of the best ways to accomplish this was by giving the boss a feeling of superiority.

> "Subordinates will tell their bosses just what
> they want to hear.  AVP Thompson with VP Snyder,
> AVP Carlson with VP Dunn, are good examples.  They
> would argue with their bosses, but let the boss
> win to build up their boss's ego.  It's incredible
> because these guys have been doing it so long, I
> don't think they even know they're doing it anymore.
> When we would come back downstairs Carlson would
> say he didn't know why he let himself get in these
> arguments with Dunn, it only gets Dunn mad; but
> everybody knows that he only gets mad if he loses
> the argument and in fact loves to win arguments.
> He wants to think that his people will be open
> with him and he also wants to be superior, thus
> losing an argument with him is th perfect way to
> get him to like you."

To keep moving up the hierarchy, the manager must show a great deal of adaptability.  In the careers of these "general managers," for the forty-one AVPs and VPs that data is available for the average number of positions was eighteen (See Chart Seven, p. 111).  This many direct bosses is a lot of adaptability in the sense of pleasing the idiosyncracies of most of them.

This practice of adapting to your superior, in some cases, in an intimate way, demanded not only self-control, but considerable political skill.  One manager said he had a "love-hate" relationship with his boss.  Hate-hate would probably have been a better description of it. The two had been put together five years ago and it only lasted a week when the subordinate was transferred.  During the fieldwork destiny put them together again.  Both were very ambitious so both needed to do a good job in their positions.  During talks with each of them and from comments they privately made to others, one could tell the tension was high.  During meetings, however, they both seemed to get along very well and even to be helpful to each other.  They were both experts at

Chart Seven:   Number of Positions

|    | AVPs   | VPs  |
|----|--------|------|
| 10 |        |      |
| 11 | X      |      |
| 12 | XX     |      |
| 13 | XXX    | XXX  |
| 14 |        |      |
| 15 | XX     |      |
| 16 | XXX    | XX   |
| 17 | XXX    | X    |
| 18 | XXXXX  |      |
| 19 |        |      |
| 20 | XXXXXX | X    |
| 21 | X      |      |
| 22 | XX     | XX   |
| 23 | XXXX   |      |

private-public boundary regulation. Their self-control had developed into strict cencorship over public expression. One division head reported, "the ones that are best at the game are sincerely supporting you in public but are the exact ones undermining you behind the scenes where the actual implementation of decisions gets done."

In another case, where it is almost unanimously agreed that the manager is very hard to work for because of his petty, critical and at times malicious behavior toward his subordinates, we find another form of adaptation. Being loyal in this case would seem difficult because of the disrespectful treatment that is returned. An AVP remarked, "There was a fella in central area who hated Resner; he later became a strong rooter of Resner. He could not give me a good rationale for this. I would say he did this because he had to survive." In an important way success at this company meant survivability, not advancement, since advancement was usually slow, and since one's chances for advancement could be damaged on any given day. Thus, surviving or staying out of trouble was the main objective.

Another individual that worked for Resner would not say anything negative about him, but when he talked about him he would call him by his first name as if he were talking about a child. Several of this individual's peers said that he "takes care of his boss" and "keeps him out of trouble." Even though his boss is still quite petty and mean to him, he has adapted by assuming a parental attitude towards his boss. One of this individual's subordinates said, "his whole life depends on his regulation of this relationship." Resner has treated this manager well in terms of bonuses over the years, thus in terms of corporate life he has been successful in the hierarchy.

In less extreme cases subordinates report other forms of showing deference by somehow expressing to the boss that his style is the best way to manage or that his values are noble. One division head remarked,

> "No matter what I do if I do not give Bently the
> impression that Bently has made a significant con-
> tribution to my management style he will not
> support me for promotion. If it is another one of
> Bently's subordinates then it might be something
> else, maybe interpersonal relations or something,
> but if he can't get credit for furthering or
> enlarging you he will not back you for promotion.
> He must be seen as contributing something, of
> making you better than you were, of taking confu-
> sion and making quality, or he won't back you.
> And I understand that Wynn is the same way."

One time I walked into the elevator and Bently was there with another one of his subordinates. The subordinate, who had been quite friendly to me during a previous interview, froze when he saw me and the look on his face begged me not to say anything. I turned and started talking to someone else and I heard the subordinate apologizing to Bently for not having his suit jacket on, since he had not known it was a "formal meeting"; Bently was wearing his jacket.

This same subordinate, about two years ago, was asked out to lunch by a female manager. He replied, "No, I'm sorry, but you know people might start talking." This year Bently decided to start helping women managers, so he told all his subordinates to start helping women managers. Thus these subordinates can now win support from Bently by helping women. This subordinate, then, gets one of his female subordi-nates a position as secretary on a committee two levels higher than her rank, a prestigious position. He also asked out to lunch the female manager that he had declined to go with two years earlier. In the past he had been known to make sexist comments, these stopped.

Another standard pattern for showing deference was loyalty. Almost everyone who talked to me told their boss they talked to me and told their boss what they talked about (probably not everything). Once when I walked up to a vice-president who had previously made some comments complimenting me to his subordinates, who was talking to one of his AVPs and to one of his division heads, both of which were good informants of mine, the resulting event took place, as recorded in my diary:

> "When I came up to Jones, Smackel, and Lacky at Lacky's cocktail party both Jones and Smackel got nervous, Jones immediately put his arms across his chest and did not make eye contact with me; Smackel talked with his hand in front of his mouth as if to guard every word. I was surprised by this since Lacky had put his arm around me when I first walked up to the three of them."

There appeared to be a high amount of paranoia regarding the relationships between the levels of the hierarchy. Perhaps the most numerous sign hanging on the walls surrounding the desks of managers on levels one and two read: "Just because you're paranoid does not mean they are not watching." A second level manager reported,

> "People around here always think that whatever they say gets back to their bosses, especially at personnel classes on management. No one really knows who has relationships with who, since everyone is always being transferred."

In a survey conducted by the company on employee attitudes results showed that the worst category was employee trust in upper management; more than seventy percent of the employees thought this was a serious problem. One AVP admitted, "People are paranoid because top management has been dishonest with them. They tell them they want them to be open, but then punish them for noncomformity."

One individual who was considered an excellent manager with a considerable amount of integrity by his peers was frozen on third level because of a conflict with a VP who was generally considered "unprincipled." This manager quit after fifteen years and opened up his own business which was doing well in the first year. A second vice-president said that the problem with this individual was that "he was not a spear carrier." This manager was independently wealthy and thus had the opportunity to quit and try his luck elsewhere. The usual situation for the non-spear carrying types is bitterness and a position on the margins of authority.

If you do not show proper deference by adapting to the emotional needs and job standards of your boss two things can happen: one, this one is for sure, you will be taken out of the promotion potential group; two, you could be punished. A division head stated,

> "If you don't play the deference game but stand up to your boss you will be yanked out of the mainstream and your career frozen. If you have angered the wrong person, you can be harassed. This is done by constant criticism of your job; information is withheld and then you're criticized for not knowing or doing something."

Sometimes a manager gets blamed for the behavior of one of his subordinates. A division head remarked, "It is standard practice to keep a subordinate away from your superior if the subordinate annoys or does not show proper respect to the superior. If you do not the superior will blame you, not only the subordinate." Another manager reported a conversation she had with her boss:

> "He told me that when I walk into an AVP meeting I should call each person "Mr. So and So" rather than by their first names even though in private I should call them by their first names. He was very

scared of them getting mad at him."

It was clear that superiors expected subordinates to behave in a particular manner. A third level manager described his fourth level boss,

> "He's a survivor, he's loose with his people—gives them credit for having intelligence—he knows enough how this organization works so that he can keep his people out of trouble by making sure Froom and Sentz get what they want. He's got the intelligence and political savvy to make fifth level. He could walk through a mine field, that's the kind of guy they like—no problems."

When I interviewed this man I heard later that he had been offended by my asking him to evaluate one of his superiors. When I said he showed no sign of being offended, the reply came, "he's a great manager."

Managers at Bell, then, are praised for running a competent organization where problems are contained therein. In interacting upwards, the manager should develop a personal relationship with his superior to win the superior's personal support. Thus bringing in new ideas, which is necessary in all organizations, becomes a complex business, since change is viewed as risky and disturbing. If you're talented enough to come up with new ideas you need another talent to market them and get credit for them. One thing that stood out at Bell is that the personal styles of most managers are conservative, not aggressive. I once asked a retired VP who had a lot to do with the promotions of the current group of top executives how come he did not promote a few risk takers into the top hierarchy. He said, "I did, Johnson, Tunney, Black and Stone are risk takers." I complained that they did not appear to be risk takers to me and he replied, "Tunney was a risk taker, he would argue with you and fight for his point of view." The message became clear: in a public monopoly, risk taking is nonconformity. The major outlook of top management is towards the perception the public has of the company and towards the measurement system; neither one of these concerns is improved by risk taking, but are improved by control, control over behavior and control over resources. There was one individual who could qualify as a risk taker—defining risk taker as one who takes deliberate actions knowing it might result in a net loss—and he was unanimously viewed as being an exception. One AVP described the situation,

> "We could only have one Bradford around here. In the old days we could only have one Aldrich around here. Don't make waves, not even ripples, is the norm. We wait until it is close to unanimous before we make a decision. Sometimes it takes ten thousand Bell managers to make one half of a decision."

It is interesting to note that Aldrich, a highly talented individual, was transferred to another Bell company in a promotion to senior vice-president. He, it is said, was too ambitious and change oriented for the CEO of that company, and is now on the sidelines at AT&T.

When individuals do come up with new ideas and are talented enough to implement them, it took yet another talent to get credit for them. There was a norm for not too aggressively taking credit for one's work. One division head was punished by an AVP for trying to sell himself too hard in order to get a transfer to a central position. Another AVP made information available to the AVP in charge of the transfer informing him that this manager was too eager to take care of himself and that he was leaving a difficult position behind for the next manager who took the job after him. The transfer was reversed. Furthermore, it was common practice for a superior to take credit for most things done in his organization. Once I mentioned to a VP that the letter explaining why he should take over another organization was well written, he replied that he wrote it, however, his AVP said he wrote it, and his division head said he wrote it. I finally heard that a district head and his people originally put together the draft. It was just about impossible to find out who really came up with an idea, usually many people worked on things and many thoughts went into them. Just the same, managers did take credit for things, sometimes things they had little to do with. On many occasions it was not the creation of an idea that people worked on, but they worked on knowing what ideas were going to be accepted and getting themselves associated with those ideas. One AVP said he was on more committees than any other AVP. I told this to another manager and he replied, "He does that not to get involved in more work, but to be able to anticipate the acceptance of ideas so as to position himself to stay out of trouble and to look like he's involved in the most important projects."

With the deference system and the information system tending to force most managers to share the credit for their ideas with their superiors and with the norm against aggressive marketing of one's accomplishments, managers tended to keep their ideas secret and tried to get things done without displaying their whole strategy. There are several other reasons this came about: one, incompetent superiors would stop projects; two, there was a norm against open conflict (see Chapter IV), and thus many projects would be stopped or sabotaged because of the negative reactions other organizations would have because of the potential loss of their resources. Therefore, manipulation became an important skill of many of the most powerful and successful managers. One division level manager explained his training,

> "My AVP would always be scheming. He used to come in and ask what plan or scheme I was working on. He always did everything in a scheme and got the rest of us to do it this way. He would also scheme with other AVPs, usually one at a time though."

Sometimes the scheme would be over and still no one knew there was a scheme. As one manager reported,

> "It's common for those guys to sit around in their offices giggling with each other about other managers taking credit for results that came about because of their scheme. Usually scheme or no scheme, things are so complex that many people had to chip in, so when ten people take credit for something most of them probably made a contribution. Most of them probably really believe it was their contribution that was most important."

The amount of scheming or any other management style that a manager used depended on who his boss was. "Managers had to act and interact differently with each one." One thing one usually did not do, however, was jump over one's boss and go to his boss without permission. A district head said,

> "I needed backing from my boss and he did not care to help or his help was so carefree that the things I wanted from human resources they would not give me. So I went to the VP to get his support. I know my boss will probably be mad and try to make life difficult for me, but if you have an incompetent boss you have to do something."

A fourth level manager, who is rated VP potential and has a job of central importance, tells that a subordinate, for the most part, only interacts with his boss and not his boss's boss. He said, "I've been in the CEO's office three times in the last five years and this is more than most other fourth levels."

Deference in modern society is not primarily found in explicit deference actions or ritual behavior where it once existed to a large degree. This is even more true in the United States where we do not have a strong aristocratic tradition. In modern society, deference is shown by what you say, what you do not say, how much you talk, how much you agree, the rules for disagreeing and contradicting, tone of voice, manner of dress, position of body, and other phenomena that are difficult for an outsider to observe because of their subtleness.

In addition to these, however, in this management system, deference is shown by adapting to the management styles, views, values, and interests of one's superior. Thus, there is a strong tendency for conformity. Without deference there is no authority, so some degree of conformity is needed for order. We see in this description of the subordinate's perception of the deference system that conformity is a ruling obsession and that values of adaptation (e.g., patronization, identification, manipulation) have grown up around it. By understanding these values we enter the conceptual world in which these managers perceive, interpret, and act. Culture is context; and it is within this context that the processes of management must be described in order for us to know these processes.

VIII. Superiors Demands on Subordinates

The other side of the deference coin from the subordinate adapting
to his superior is the superior's demands on the subordinate. If these
two parts are not in harmony then the deference system breaks down and
authority is lost. As we saw in the last section, the deference system
has many parts, some of which are explicitly expected (loyal reporting
of information) and some implicitly expected (manipulation of information to affect change). In this section the cultural structure of the
dominating part of the deference system will be examined.

To begin with, we will look at the individual managers who set the
tone for the deference system. They set the tone because they were the
ones most responsible for promotions in the 1950s and 1960s, thus it
was towards them that the ambitious young managers would be oriented.
Herman Keech came to work for the telephone company in 1924. He was a
powerful vice-president of human resources from 1950 to 1967. Another
VP who worked with him in those days remarked, "He was incredibly loud,
always yelling, even when he was on the phone in his office I could
hear him talking as if he was sitting across from me in my office"
(their offices were thirty yards apart). He promoted, with the guiding
approval of the senior vice-president, John Mathews, whom will be
discussed next, most of the VPs and AVPs in office today.

A manager who had recently been hired into the AVP level reported
that he had heard others, when speaking of Keech, refer to him as "The
Czar." A VP, when I brought up Keech's name, said, "he's a piece of
machinery." Another VP remarked that Keech "scared the hell out of you."
A third level manager, when speaking of Keech, elaborated,

> "When you passed him in the hall or saw him on the
> elevator hello was quite remarkable for him to say.
> The secret of success in those days was not to have
> a personal point of view. Allegiance was built
> into the manager in the old way. Immediately when
> there was any criticism it would be interpreted as
> an implied disloyalty. When I do interviews today
> for company publications people, even most friends,
> are careful what they say."

That managers had been trained not to speak up is undoubtedly
true. At a yearly conference in 1980 all the VPs and AVPs got together
for a meeting to set policy and plans for the upcoming months. The
relatively new CEO, new compared to the twenty-five to thirty years of
working together most other managers attending had experienced, was
asking for ideas and opinions on certain problems that demanded a new
approach to solving. One AVP stated, "This is the first time I ever
saw the group get bitchy with each other." The bitchiness probably
had come about from the managers having been put in the position of
having to participate rather than having been told what to do. One
AVP, the only Jew, stood up and said to the CEO, "It's your decision
on restructuring and everyone in this room has a hidden agenda—their
own needs and security—and can't make the decision." The AVP reported,
"after the meeting a dozen managers came up to me and said I said it
the way it should be said." Two other managers stood up and supported
this AVP, both engineers, one of them said, "After I stood up and
spoke at the conference, I got a half-dozen phone calls commending me
for doing this—this is a sign that people don't feel free to speak
up."

Not only are managers expected not to speak up, but as a third
level manager remarked, "Most talented, ambitious people, here, grovel

as part of their career development." During the days of Keech and SVP
Westover the domination from the top was probably worse. In the
1950s and 1960s, all four line VPs had drivers for their cars; now just
the SVP and the CEO have drivers. Furthermore, there was a special
elevator and elevator operator, which no longer exists, "waiting to
whisk the VPs to the eighteenth floor."

Bell managers were taught not to participate but to obey. Managers
that tried to participate were considered unsually strong. A district
head, in discussing an individual who was tenacious in his work to get
new programs instituted, said, "He's got brass balls, he goes over
there and won't give up until they have at least tried his idea."
Another district head added, "Brass balls is about the only profanity I
ever heard at Bell." The norm against conflict was strong and the
pressure to conform was equally as strong. One manager who has worked
for three other large corporations reported, "Seymour Ikes divorced his
wife and married another woman; this impacted his career. This kind of
extra business social behavior is not looked upon as good at Bell."
What is looked upon as good at Bell is the idea of a model citizen.
Bell managers were encouraged to act like model citizens. A third
level manager said, "Bell people always step aside to let others go
ahead, we are willing waiters in line. I could tell on the steet who
is going to come into this building." A fourth level manager added,

> "My boss would always open doors for his subordi-
> nates, you don't see this in other industries, so
> now I do the same. A few years ago they had to
> send notices around to tell the men in the front
> in the elevator not to try and step aside to let
> the women out, but to get out first."

Well maybe you do not see this in other industries, but nonetheless lurking behind the Bell managers' politeness was a strict authoritative code for conformity and obedience. A third level manager explained, "When a superior confronts his subordinate it usually reduces them to ashes; this makes their behavior predictable." The purpose of the strict deference system was to tighten up control. A top down hierarchy evolved because the top management was primarily concerned with public image. The Bell manager should be "A hail fellow well met, the pillar of the community." Or, in the words of another, "the salt of the earth, honest, dedicated, and loyal." And the deference system was the major instrument for achieving and maintaining this behavior. As noted in the last section, again here from another informant, "You're only supposed to talk to people who are on your own level." Deference from the bottom meant control from the top.

If one did not fit in he was weeded out; either one did not come to begin with, quit, or sat on the sidelines. Many people that were promoted were not strong willed people. This was not true on the VP level where obstinancy seemed to be a fundamental qualification for office; but on the AVP level and below the ranks were filled with "good soldiers." A VP, an AVP, a division head, and a district head all said the same thing: "There are lost of insecure people around." The district head went on to say, "My boss once would not give me an opinion until he heard his boss's opinion." This was typical at this telephone company.

The stories told about SVP Mathews, who later became CEO from 1965 to 1970, express even better the temper of the ruling side of the deference system. Mathews might have picked up his style from the preceding generation. One AVP said, "We were afraid of Mathews and of Godfrey who came before him" (CEO from 1949 to 1965). Another AVP, chuckling the whole say through, tells the following stories about Mathews:

> "Stone ran an employee attitude survey and it showed that it would be a good idea for the CEO to talk to low level employees across the state. Mathews was so bad at this that when he did it there were hundreds of complaints, mostly from women. He was asked a question in [a city] about promoting women into middle management. He responded, 'This company has been good to women. I see them taking vacations in Hawaii and Bermuda, wearing minks, and some even have new cars. Other than that I think women should keep a low profile or just stay at home in the kitchen.' Well, you can imagine how this would upset the women but Mathews didn't care."

> "Nobody really liked Mathews when he was SVP and we were glad when be became CEO. The problem was he got worse when be became CEO because he still tried to get involved in all the details of operations. One year when we went up to Summit Hill he got up and started talking. He was upset that he set a 8.14 return objective and we were only at 7.46. He said, 'I told you that you were bringing too many people to work here. Now until we reach 8.14, every one of your jobs is hot secure.' He told one manager to drive home with him and two weeks later Benson was transferred to Texas."

> "Once McMillan disagreed with Mathews and McMillan was retired. One thing about Mathews, he set the policy. He made policy decisions and everybody knew it. Last year one AVP did not get a raise and he called up the CEO and went and talked to him about it. This CEO is a gentleman and would hear him out. If you would have called Mathews up complaining about something he did he would tell you if you don't like it leave, don't bother me again, talk to your boss."

This same manager said, "Mathews was a good wrestler and he had been captain of the wrestling team in college;" another AVP stated, "Mathews had been a great wrestler in college and won the NCWA wrestling association championship at the 145 pound class." When I asked Mathews about his wrestling accomplishments he replied, "I never wrestled in my life, I played football, I was a half-back." The fact that these two managers made this mistake pointed toward an image of the center of authority as a lone fighting champion. Mathews, as the core symbol of the charismatic authority that ordered collective action, represented demands for deference based on superiority, danger, and above all the power to control.

The CEO before Mathews was "basically a salesman." He concentrated his efforts on the company's relations with the community, however, as reported above he also struck fear in the minds of his subordinates. A retired AVP recalled the Summit Hill conference during Godfrey's tenure,

> "He used to rally the troops and get them organized at Summit. Also he would use Summit to cuss people out. At half-time during the golf tournament he used to give a pep talk. He was a great leader. Both him and Mathews ran a tight conference up there. VPs and AVPs used to spend weeks getting their presentations ready, scared that they would be picked apart. It used to be tense up there."

A VP added, "The management team has been traumatized, twenty years ago at Summit if you made a mistake you could lose your job."

The CEO that came in after Mathews, in 1970, was one of the indivi- duals who was hired after the war. Thus he had been a peer of the other VPs and AVPs. For here it will be sufficient to state that during his tenure "no coffee was consumed on the eighteenth floor because he did not drink it. If you wanted a cup of coffee, whether vice-president or secretary, you had to go down to the seventeenth floor to drink it."

Even if these strict standards of conformity had their benefits in predictability, they had their costs also. A division head stated,

> "As you move up the line you don't give and get
> critical feedback and you get rewarded, so you stay
> this way. If I come up to my subordinates and ask
> them for feedback on my performance, I will not get
> a good evaluation. We are all suspicious of the
> feedback we get."

Hence one of the problems with strong demands for deference is that it diminishes the ability for accurate appraisal and open discussion. When criticism, even honest criticism, is considered disloyal, then the deference system is interfering with the ability of managers to communicate and dysfunctional behavior results.

Dysfunction to some, however, is functional for others. Some individuals developed "a totally political style." That is, their only concern was with pleasing superiors. The advantage of this to top management is that they can increase, through these individuals, their span of control. When I was in the field I noticed that an important committee was chaired by a "turkey," a manager who is "at best put up with" by his peers. The apparent benefit of this strategy is that he would not let the committee do anything that was not first approved by his superiors. The problem it created, however, is that it slowed down the work of the committee and it demoralized the subcommittee members who did the committee's research. Top management was more interested in control than they were in the output of the committee; many company publications were produced telling of the importance of the committee, showing pictures of its members, and discussing its purpose in a grand way, yet the chairman's vital concern was with "touching all bases."

In this kind of social system where a strong emphasis is placed on deference, the behavior of both the superior and the subordinate is limited. The ambitious subordinate must play a socially established role and the superior must demand the role be played or else he is not playing his role. The result is a rigid behavioral system where the organization is not responsive or flexible. Creativity is kept to a minimum and risk takers are bred out. Status pride is the ruling obsession not individual pride; status pride demands a form of public recognition which is only given for performing to a socially acceptable standard. Status pride and individual pride are the two end points on a continuum. What is being said here is that status pride is dominant in this organization: Looking good is better than doing good.

IX. Conclusion

At this company career development meant the manager's path in relation to the center of authority. For a career to "develop" meant that an individual moved from one formal position in the division of labor to another. A successful career development was one where a manager moved closer toward the center of authority, thus increasing his power and status. In terms of the formal hierarchy, a successful career meant moving upward into increasingly less populated levels of management and gaining more general rights and responsibilities. This moving through formal positions, however, was primarily controlled by the informal system of action. And the informal system of action was constituted by personal relationships. Thus, it depended on the manager's personal ties to determine his movement within the formal hierarchy.

Therefore, the nature of authority--the legitimate power to influence the actions of others--is primarily charismatic at this company. Managers were awarded and punished not primarily by following rules and regulations, nor by unquestioned habits that had long been the traditional mode of operation, but by the belief in the awe-arousing centrality of individuals with order creating power. Ultimately this authority originated with the CEO, but then spread out through the levels of the hierarchy establishing an informal distribution of power that was based on personal ties.

The individuals with power derived from their closeness to the center of authority were obeyed because they wielded the ability to make decisions that could change the structure of the company or a manager's place in it. Charisma was imputed to these individuals. Career development, when it was successful, meant that managers had been chosen by central figures of authority to be given positions that were deemed important by these authorities. This formal position inspired others to attribute charisma to these managers because it meant that they were personally approved of by the higher authorities, thus sharing in their power and status. In this way the institutional charisma was dispersed to structure the distribution of power. Furthermore, by choosing individuals for these positions who were personally acceptable, control was maintained over which individuals received order creating capacities.

This intense reliance on personal relationships led to a tendency to choose managers who had a certain type of personal characteristics. Hence, ambitious managers adapted to this situation by conforming to these social qualities that had proven to be successful. The ability to adapt was, however, limited by the sexual and racial standards that were applied a priori to all personal-professional relationships. Women and blacks, for example, were forbidden from upper levels of management. The general demographic patterns that were approved of were, almost to the man, male caucasions with Protestant or Catholic religious backgrounds. But this was just the prescreening mechanisms that were more or less taken for granted.

The more detailed screening mechanisms were categories for appropriate behavior. It was only within terms of these categories that personal ties were vertically maintained. If a manager was eager to gain status by moving into central positions that enabled him to exercise charismatic authority, he would have to adapt to the personal demands of a superior. The superior, on the other hand, would have to choose which managers he would support. He had a number of subordinates adapting their personal-management styles to win his support. Much of this interpersonal maneuvering was based on the superior's demands for deference. Also, it depended on the subordinate's ability to contribute to the success of the superior, since the superior inevitably was also being judged by his superior. Thus, the two key components in winning support from one's boss was usefulness and deference signalling. Ultimately, deference signalling was the most important component because several managers would be useful and instrumentally talented, thus seductive or interpersonal skills proved to be the component that solidified the personal relationship with the superior.

The central category in this culture of deference demands was conformity. Within the category of conformity each superior carved out his own priorities for just how conformity was to be measured. Hence, it was the manager's ability to adapt to the continuing variability of deference demands that ultimately insured his advancement toward the center of authority and into its charismatic instilling central structure.

## ENDNOTES

1. Thomas Cochran has argued that the needs of business have been the prime influence in the development of American culture and that culture in twentieth century America is becoming more uniform due to a developing uniformity in business. Business in American Life: A History (New York: McGraw Hill Book Company, 1972). Thus, perhaps this tension will ease as the category of status becomes more based on group attachment as large bureaucracies continue to dominate American life. But, as will be seen in this research, a considerable attachment to the belief in individualism is still distinct in American bureaucracy.

2. Gary Willis, "The Kennedy Imprisonment," The Atlantic Monthly, (January and February, 1982).

3. Thomas Cochran, Personal Communication, Radnor, Pennsylvania, February, 1982.

4. Ibid.

5. Willis, "The Kennedy Imprisonment."

6. Max Weber, From Max Weber: Essays in Sociology (New York: Oxford University Press, 1946).

7. Edward Shils, "Charisma, Order, and Status," in Center and Periphery: Essays in Macrosociology (Chicago: University of Chicago Press, 1975).

8. Ibid.

9. "Middle Management Succession," Bell Company, 1980.

10. Ibid.

11. Ibid.

12. Ibid.

13. Ibid.

14. Ibid.

# Chapter IV

THE QUALITY OF COOPERATION

I.  Introduction

There is no possibility of understanding cooperation in this
company without understanding conflict.[1]  Even though cooperation must
frame the original impulse for collective effort, and even though the
final result must be a cooperative one, in between these two points
ambiguous information, varying alternatives, questions of power, and
contradictions of interest must be temporarily settled to arrive at
action based on common purpose.  To do this is no small matter; it is
the essence of management.

Cooperation is the joint action of at least two individuals based
on an agreement of expectations.  Conflict is the opposed actions of
at least two individuals based on incompatible expectations.  At this
company we will see that there was no way, given the social structure
or the cultural tendencies—either one was enough, together they constructed the information and its understanding that framed each situation—to arrive at cooperative action without working through a certain amount of (depending on the issue) conflict.

This chapter will focus on the qualitative patterns found in the
cooperative interaction of the thirty-seven assistant vice presidents
(AVPS).  This will facilitate our study of the cooperative process,
since all AVPs are of the same formal rank, the complicating issue of
formal authority will be minimized.  The cooperative process will be
characterized by a detailed description of the social structural and
cultural influences that combine to give it its particular shape.

133

First, the social patterns that provide the basis for the context in which the cooperative process must be carried out will be discussed. Second, an important permanent committee will be analyzed to find out what function formal structures play in the cooperative process on the AVP level. Third, an analysis into the informal processes that have developed to facilitate cooperation will be presented. Finally, a meeting between the staff coalition and the line coalition in which a transfer of resources took place will be described. This meeting will be used to demonstrate the role of conflict in the cooperative process.

## II. The Basis of Cooperation

Unlike the church which most members are born into and unlike the army where members have been traditionally forced into involvement, the industrial organization usually attracts its would-be members by their voluntary choice. In Chapter III we saw that this utility had traditionally meant secure employment, security through benefits, and stability because of its monopolistic position. Hence, people who valued security and stability over risk and uncertainty would find this utility to offer an employment structure to fit their wants. It follows that the cooperative processes of a group of people who preferred security and stability would be influenced accordingly. Indeed this is what was found. Except for the individuals whose main interest was power, certainly not the majority, the AVPs were mostly "good soldiers." Also, an important factor influencing this behavior was that almost all the AVPs were in their mid-fifties, and most felt that they had little opportunity for advancement. Thus, cooperation at this company had a "no waves" glossing to it, since many individuals were inclined to seek security, and since ambition was tempered by a perceived lack of upward mobility.

Paralleling these personal factors, the organization formally encouraged the idea of employee safety and teamwork. Instead of promoting the "fight and get ahead" idea of work, the company promoted the "do it for the company and community" idea of work. Thus, there was also a "dedication" glossing to interpersonal efforts. In this section we will describe the general sociological reasons for a conflict averse and personally attached part to the cooperative process.

The Bell managers had traditionally seen their company as being "all things to all people." Cost was not a major consideration. If someone wanted phone service and lived five miles from a road, twenty miles from their nearest neighbor, they would get it, no matter the quarter of a million dollars installation price. And their monthly bill would be the same as everyone else's—about eight dollars. This was the idea of universal service. Costs were averaged across the whole universe of customers. Upon this framework the communication system of the United States, probably the finest in the world, was built. Along with "all things to all people," the phrase "little old lady in tennis shoes" was another image that was used by managers to describe their customers. It was used not just to capture a reading of their idea of service to the community (it is important to note that this image pictured the community as vulnerable and dependent), but to capture a reading about how they themselves felt about their work and saw their performance of it (they were the all things and they were the servers of the little old ladies). Part of this was propaganda used to justify the protected position of a legal monopoly. But part of it, the more important part, was a heartfelt need to be a part of a community, a part which made a contribution to the strength of the community. A part of most Bell managers glorified in community service; it balanced not only their individual need to be recognized, but, as we will see, their fear of loss.

This all came together at Bell in the cooperative effort. A regulatory AVP described his experience:

> "The people are great to work with, the level of
> dedication to the task that Bell people have I

most admire. It's my duty, they don't go at it in
a negative way. It's fun to be part of this, it's
almost contagious and self snowballing, it's a
satisfying experience."

Most of the AVPs seemed to be welded into this conception of coopera-

tion. Indeed, after thirty years they knew little else. An engineering

AVP stated why he came to Bell:

"In the signal corps I worked on the Manhatten
Project, then I went to the Pentagon and worked on
a secret telecommunications project. Most people
on this project were from Bell and I really liked
them, they were friendly, helpful, congenial, easy
to get along with, so I went looking for Bell. I
had better offers but thought Bell presented
opportunity for my interests and I liked what I
saw of Bell people."

It was the willingness to work together (precisely the opposite of what

we found with the VPs) that made this organization attractive to the

would-be AVPs. Indeed, one talented AVP who had a chance to be a VP

turned away from this path because "he didn't like the people."

Most of these managers came to Bell just after being involved in a

massive cooperative effort: the United States armed forces. Coming to

Bell was not all that different: all male upper management, strict

hierarchy, demands for deference, monopolistic organizational structure,

etc. What is even more striking in regards to similarity with the

armed forces is the concept of employee service that was designed and

developed to complement the idea of universal service. In the armed

forces one is asked to risk one's life in service of one's country.

At this utility the concept of service was officially discussed in a

way that implied that the manager was expected to go that far if need

be. And not just at work, but being a Bell employee, he should serve

his community generally to such a degree. In the company's one hundred and three year history, one hundred and forty-six employees have received a company sponsored bronze medal for "acts of heroism that result in the saving of a human life."[2] "Another fifteen...received silver...awards for nationally noteworthy acts of public service."[3] Within this official context of the idea of service and with images of paternal strength and dedication provoked by viewing customers as a "little old lady in tennis shoes," it can be seen that cooperative behavior had more than economic and political motivation. Being a Bell manager, in part, meant being a community-minded, dedicated, loyal individual. Cooperation was focused by this meaning and cooperative action usually carried this significance. It, no doubt, carried egotistical ambition also, but it is just this complexity of varying, sometimes contradictory, meanings that makes social action in need of analysis to be understood.

Now we are in a position to discuss what brought these personalities to this culture. A striking pattern emerged from the biographical interviews. Thirteen biographical interviews were conducted on the AVP level. Eight out of the thirteen had traumatic events in their family history or when answering the question of earliest memory or an important event from childhood called up painful experiences. Here in brief form is a summary of that data:

AVP One:

> "My parents were divorced when I was eleven,
> right after the war. An important event from
> childhood was my uncle and aunt breaking up due
> to the war. Another important event was coming
> home from work and seeing my uncle who had just
> died in a farming accident."

To another question on why he came to work for Bell he replied,

"Because you could see them making an investment
in you. That was a hard decision because offers
from other corporations were higher, it was not
a money factor. Secure foundations for the
employee for the future, very employee oriented,
not a statistic, but you were joining another
family.

AVP Two:

"My mother's father died early in her life. She
was raised by aunts and uncles. I don't have the
slightest idea what happened to her mother."

AVP Three:

"My father was raised in an orphanage."

AVP Four:

"My father worked for Bell. He died in 1941. I
started working for Bell in 1941, right out of
high school and the tail end of the depression.
Many times back early I was going to quit. I was
supporting a widowed mother, baby sister, baby
brother, I needed more money. I was going to quit
but my mother told me not to. My mother had a
brother who was a lineman. Benefits, treatments,
vacations were good."

AVP Five:

"My oldest sister raised us. My mother died when
I was nine."

AVP Six:

"We were quite poor. My father died when I was
four. My earliest memory was setting the house
on fire when I was three."

AVP Seven:

"My earliest memory, I was about four years old, I
wanted to go downstairs and join my family, I
thought they were eating ice cream, I was not
allowed."

AVP Eight:

"An important event from my childhood was stomach
pains I used to get in first grade when my dad

drove me to start school."

Furthermore, out of the three biographical interviews conducted on the VP level, one VP reported a traumatic childhood experience resulting in the loss of his father.

In addition to these eight AVPs, two out of the five other AVPs given biographical interviews mentioned that the weakest aspect of their management style was their "reluctance to deal with conflict" or they were "too permissive" a manager. Two of the eight above also mentioned "difficulty correcting faults of subordinates" and being "too easy and understanding" with subordinates. Hence, there was a tendency for individuals who shied away from conflict to be attracted to the utility.

From this data it can be concluded that there was a general pattern of individuals whose childhoods were disturbed in terms of a sense of unity or security to be attracted to the stability, security, and sense of belonging that characterized this public utility. Many individuals that came to this utility were inclined to avoid conflict in their relationships because they felt that their relationships, in general, were of a tenuous nature.[4] When one joined this utility they were making the best guarantee of long-term economic security that was possible given the information of corporate survivability that was available. In addition, the reputation for being an employer that was sensitive to employee needs and the sense of mission derived from the strong emphasis on public service, both provided a context in which an individual inclined to make a personal attachment to an industrial organization and its corporate purpose was encouraged. Indeed, "Ma

Bell" was the only public corporation in the United States that explicitly cultivated a sense of belonging based on strong employee economic protection and moral selfworth.  An AVP put it this way:

> "We're not making some sleezy product.  What we're
> doing is an important service to the community at
> a good price."

Perhaps the managers did not feel more aggressive than their counterparts in other corporations, but they did feel that they were doing an important job and they derived their self-worth from it.

Thus, there were strong influences on the cooperative process for teamwork.  Satisfaction from belonging to a morally valuable production process influenced managers to avoid conflict.  And even though there were other influences influencing contrary motivations, there remained a certain degree of "consensus management" throughout the AVPs' interactions.  A regulation AVP reported:

> "Decisions are usually made following group dis-
> cussion; in airing out pros and cons, risks,
> penalty evaluation, much discussion, then group
> consensus."

It was unusual for conflict to break out in the open.  A staff AVP said,

> "We have a low tolerance for conflict, we avoid
> confrontation, it's unpleasant to correct or
> criticize."

A division head added, "If you don't confront people you don't hurt them.  Confrontation is uncomfortable."  Most managers were not aggressive and thought it dangerous to be aggressive.  Out of the thirty-seven AVPs, no more than four were considered outspoken and aggressive.  One of these four mentioned,

> "There's a great fear of me in my group of peers
> and superiors.  I am a thorn in the side of the
> group.  I don't play the game.  They fear me

because I tell the truth, I'm unpredictable and
this is a source of power for me."

The "truth" that he was talking about was nothing more than his opinion.
The others did not have opinions or if they did they did not mention
them. Managers went along with what was told them. A legal AVP said,

"There are a couple leaders, but the rest are
putting their time in the company and to the
degree that they have a vision they won't risk
telling it."

A culture that encouraged consensus and conformity rather than
initiative and independence to this degree would inevitably lead to
problems in the area of decision making. A staff AVP described,

"The organization does not communicate very well
and we have trouble being decisive. We will lean
one way or the other on issues without any firm
commitment to yes or no. This happens because
issues are not clear and it is not clear what is
the right decision."

There were not many, if any, individuals that were inclined to make
decisions in an uncertain world. A marketing AVP agreed,

"We want things in black and white, we try to make
things into simple absolutes. They don't want
to make judgements, this is a problem throughout
the corporation. This permeates our engineering
group. They want a forecast that is accurate;
this worked under a monopoly, but won't work in a
competitive environment."

These ideas of waiting for near certainty and group agreement were a
time consuming process. Managers were described as "drags things on
forever" or "always looking for the middle of the road." The monopoly
culture discouraged action. A district head analyzed,

"AVPs try to be the first to interpret new legis-
lation to their VP. You try to produce a white
paper. You'll have five people submitting an
interpretation on issues that are too voluminous
for him to read or too complex for him to under-

stand. Many of the issues that are facing the
company are viewed to be very complex and hard to
dissect. I have found these white papers as in
fact getting an issue to an understandable level,
but nothing gets done, analysis is excitement,
action is overlooked."

Indeed it seemed that most managers were analyzing and not acting.

Many personalities seemed like they would support little else. The

impression that an observer was given was that the staff management

system, for the most part, was designed to look busy, collect data,

present the data, but little more. A division head stated,

"There is not a reward in this business for
decisiveness. People brag about strategies for
avoiding decisions."

This lack of follow through in the decision process inevitably led

to boredom and laziness. The AVPs, by their own estimates, figured

that between fifteen to sixty-five percent of their peers did not work

hard. An accounting AVP explained,

"There are eight to ten lazy department heads
[AVPs]. Better but need improvement are twenty
more."

A regulation AVP put it this way:

"Thirty percent are not working hard. We don't
have a way to get people off the payroll. We
don't have options to cut the work load, so we
share the work load."

Another regulation AVP added,

"There is a disapportionment of job tasks. Some
department heads have tremendously a lot to do
while others have much less. At least twenty-five
percent don't work hard. We need a mix of ages on
all levels, this would create more competition."

A marketing AVP remarked,

"Twenty percent (8) don't put in a good day's work.
They are coasting along. This problem is not

talked about. Occasionally it is mentioned in
connection with an individual."

A staff AVP gave his view:

"Age has had an impact on them. No more upward
mobility or no more money making potential. It's
a life problem that is reinforced by the corporation: staying there until you retire. Thus, one
chooses the course of action that is least painful.
This is a big problem. We will have to learn to
deal with this."

It appeared that this "big problem" was not only not discussed in
the company, but was not even known to many of the managers that were
perceived as "coasting along." One AVP who was fearful of the harmful
effects of my research gave the following example of people getting
hurt:

"A proportion of the fifth level hardly do any
work. And if you document this then it will shock
these people like falling out of bed. They will
be able to see themselves like others see them and
this is not always good, it could be destructive."

There did seem to be a degree of illusion surrounding some of the
AVPs. One AVP was working on a crossword puzzle on two separate occasions when I walked into his office. Both times he slowly slid the
puzzle out of my view as if I did not see him working on it. This
same AVP when looking over an outline I had drawn up of my research
activities after about five months in the field said, "When you uncover
rocks and shine a light underneath them, you'll find worms and moles."
There were no strict standards for work output, thus individuals, over
the years, floated into positions of little work. No one said anything
about it to them because "confrontation was unpleasant," so they saw
others as not working hard but were able to ignore their own output.
An accounting AVP concluded, "One thing that is wrong is that there

are no penalties for anything."

The cooperative process, then, affected individuals in certain ways but not in others. It made one feel like one belonged to a group, but it did not make one feel like one had to perform to a certain standard. It gave one a sense of moral responsibility, but it did not give one a sense of managerial responsibility: If one took a public action it must be just, but if one did not take actions, the business would work around their silence.

The AVPs were a "club"; if one belonged he was taken care of. An engineering AVP replied,

> "You join a club, an exclusive club. Made up of 44. You're very conscious of joining this club. Rarely do anger or disagreements go below this level. They don't bring it up where subordinates are present. You hold it until you are sitting down with Black, for example."

An accounting AVP added,

> "It's an interesting club. You can't attack fifth level because we protect each other. A lot of fourth levels can't get things done so they go to their fifth level which goes to another fifth level and gets it done."

The AVPs were in a structurally important position. They were below the ineffective officer group and above a considerably younger core fourth level group. They were the company's main mechanism for minimizing conflict. They isolated the officers, controlled the subordinates, and got along with each other. And they did so by avoiding confrontation. But the conflict was there even if it was not allowed to break out into the open. A human resources AVP, with an alarmed expression, stated that the biggest worry that the AVPs had about my research was that I would tell an AVP what I heard about him and he would know who told me. Hence, the AVPs knew that there were many tensions between them, and they thought they knew who thought what about who, but all these negative social feelings were kept tightly controlled through norms against open expression. This norm was expressed by the fact that when I interviewed the AVPs, they, almost down to the man, were very eager to discuss their relationships, but at meetings when a group of them were present they would just say hello, so that they would not be accused of being one of the ones who was "talking," or in need of a "father confessor," or having "diarrhea of the mouth." It was a certain tension that they lived with every day, but never fully accepted as expressed by their eagerness to break the rules and discuss these matters in confidence with me.

The result of this cooperative behavior on the AVP level was to keep the AVPs safe from the VPs wrath by collectively screening information they got, and to keep their division heads out of trouble by individually not delegating any considerable authority. One high rated division head complained of the "clear line drawn between the top sixty and below. The line drawn between fifth and sixth is not as broad as the line drawn between fifth and fourth." The fifth level managers were a "club" and therefore kept fairly strong boundaries on both sides. If they did not, then the "club" could not exist. Another division head remarked,

> "If I was fifth level, I would do differently from
> most fifth levels, I would be out with the troops.
> Having staff meetings, active participant, more
> forceful and participative."

This was not usually done on the AVP level because cooperation meant getting your work completed in as non-conflict, self-advantageous a way as possible, and because charging up the "troops" would inevitably lead to conflict with other organizations. This ruled out hard driving participative type managers. A division head described,

> "Almost all fifth levels are good soldiers. There is a mixture of self-preservation and duty."

Another division head agreed,

> "We have people who are not risk takers, people who will protect their interests. Nice, safe people, who know their place, who won't blow the whistle."

The cooperative process on the AVP level was a mixture of low keyed individualism, common needs for security, and a division of labor that was more designed for control than accomplishment. "Problems" were abhorred and on the AVP level one could expect cooperation in handling them. Initiatives were another story. There was a reluctance to get involved in action that was not directed toward solving something that was agreed to be wrong. The phrase, "Don't fix it if it ain't broken" was not an uncommon remark. One division head complained, "I send things up and never get any response back." For most managers, initiatives were risky and risk was seen more as dangerous than potentially rewarding.

Another major characteristic of the AVP group which had an impact on the quality of their cooperative interaction was the degree to which they knew each other. An engineering AVP replied, "We have grown up together. We can read each other without thinking about it." Indeed they did know each other well. After twenty-five to thirty-five years of working together their thoughts about each other were thick with memories that could be called up to understand a particular action or

an expected response that one was going to make. Another engineering
AVP stated,

> "All have a certain amount of intelligence,
> aggressiveness and ruthlessness. With Breecher
> I have to show him that there is something in
> his self-interest to get him to do anything.
> Some you can deal with straight-forward, others
> you have to sit down with a cup of coffee and
> discuss football scores first."

The point is that each one knew fairly well how to "deal with" the
other.

In fact knowing one another was a big part of what the cooperative
process was all about. "Bill won't sponsor your research because he's
insecure." "Tom, he'll tell you everything--he's a bucket mouth."
"Greg won't let you near his people because he's paranoid of anybody
knowing anything about his shop." "Tim will talk in technicalities, he
won't be up front." "Charley won't talk personalities, he'll want to
keep everything general." "Jim will level with you, you'll get some
good information from him." And so on. But of course there were
surprises. Bob, who was not supposed to talk, did; and Kevin, who was
not supposed to be a "blushing violet", was. All in all, however,
their descriptions of each other were impressively consistent.

Of course these descriptions were more than mechanisms for predic-
tion; they were also descriptions of themselves: expressions of an
intricate web of emotional attachments. They were pictures of loyalty:
"Mack and Fenton started together in the early days. Mack broke his
leg and Fenton helped him once." They were pictures of affection:

> "Years ago I used to walk to the train station
> in the morning. Many times Morrison would be
> driving to work and would pick me up. When he did
> it would be a tremendous amount of fun. We would

> never go the same way. If a light turned red,
> Morrison would turn, constantly turning all over
> the place. We would end up in all parts of the
> city. This was great fun and Morrison was great."

Some of them liked each other and some of them did not, but the expression of strong emotions were kept under control no matter if they were positive or negative. As we will see later in this chapter, these feelings of trust, loyalty, respect, honor, etc. were used to construct extensive informal networks for information processing and collective action.

Another reason they were keenly aware of each other other than the shared experiences was, as we saw in Chapter II, they were very similar in regards to age, race, sex, religion, and socio-economic position. A third level woman observed,

> "All six company managers living in center city
> are black or white female. No white male district
> level or above [about 700 managers] live in
> center city."

Another commonality was their attitude toward children. Out of the thirty-two AVPs that data was obtained for, all but one had children. Five had five children; six had four children; eight had three children; eleven had two children; and one had one child.

When they got together before meetings there were comments about their children, discussions of sports, comments on hobbies (growing flowers was a hobby that occupied at least six of them), jokes of a sexual nature ("Who moved my bag" brought the response "Haven't you had your bag pushed around before" [punning on his briefcase]), and discussions on activities appropriate to the age group (What's the Y's exercise program for the fifty to sixty year olds like?"). And of course there was golf. Sometimes these different areas were intermixed as when, in at least two different meetings, a division head and an AVP joked about whose "blooms" were bigger. Also, as was noted in Chapter II, they seemed to have a common orientation towards women.[5] Here is an interaction that took place when the only woman at a profit planning board meeting went up to the chairman to tell him the plan for lunch:

> "When Froom went up to Weiner after the CPC meeting to tell him he was supposed to eat lunch downstairs and come back to the conference room after lunch, he looked uncomfortable. He crossed his arms across his chest, looked a bit dismayed, indignant, and said, "I wanted a working lunch, I didn't expect this split, I didn't want a split, no one told me about any split." [The look on his face was one of slightly annoyed humor.]

Another AVP, this time an operations manager, also expressed confusions when descibing his subordinates. First, he said three out of six of his district heads were female. When I asked for their names he changed it to eight district heads and one of them was female and she had three men reporting to her. A female middle manager summed up the situation:

> "Most men have subservient wives, daughters, mothers and then they meet professional women and they don't know how to act."

Women managers complained of AVPs and VPs meeting them on the street and kissing them on the cheek, putting their arms around them, calling them "honey," "sweetheart," or "dear." It was a case of the men not having had to interact with female middle managers for the first two decades of their careers. When many of them did have to interact, it was a confusing experience for them.

Thus we have seen that cooperation between the AVPs was based on a variety of feelings and beliefs that structured their interaction. They all shared, for the most part, a certain amount of dedication to the purpose of a public utility, dispositions to avoid conflict and confrontation, needs for occupational security, desires for a familial organization (fear of loss), preference for group decision making, inclination to follow orders and avoid risk, desires to avoid the corporate "rat race," avoid initiative, similar interests and backgrounds in terms of social and cultural beliefs, and an extensive knowledge of each other's personal propensities. Finally, we come to the last major theme in the cooperative interaction of the AVPs, but certainly not the least important: competition. A division head remarked,

> "A lot of egos are involved. These guys were recognized as quality people to get to this level and thus can't be shown up without losing face. There is a strong dislike for each other sometimes because of competition."

This "strong dislike" was kept much better in check on the AVP level than on the VP level. A division head reported,

> "The AVPs pride themselves on not having petty, trivial, competitive battles like the officers. They feel someone has to run the company."

None-the-less competitive impulses were certainly in existence. When an AVP asked me if I ever thought how golf tells one about the company culture, I replied that I had heard that a past CEO said that he could tell more about an individual on the golf course than anywhere else. To this he responded:

> "How could you find out more about a man on the golf course with his $250 golf clubs, his expensive shoes, than you could with a runner wearing $25 worth of stuff when he is running with himself

and the elements and nothing else.  A fucking golf
game, what a joke.  I could be a great golfer if
I put the time and effort into training for it."

An interesting aspect of the competitive interaction between the

AVPs was that it was usually subtle and, for the men, such an extensive

part of their work life that they took it for granted.  None of them

ever mentioned it during interviews on management practices.  But the

women did.  A female middle manager analyzed:

"The meetings with men are a kind of mating ritual.
Small talk, play a card, then someone else will
play a card.  Old power play, can I win my point?
They keep an ace up their sleeve.  At meetings
they play to power.  VP Kent would have monthly
meetings on television.  If Kent was in the west,
the western people will be aggressive, if he
is in the east, the eastern group will be more
aggressive."

"If my boss calls a meeting, I know the first ten
minutes will be about sports or something (How's
your son doing at college?).  The approach is for
men to have a hidden agenda, never say everything
at once.  If I give this will he give that.  Men
act this way because they have been taught to do
this.  They watched their superiors do it.  Out-
smart your adversary."

This guardedness was not just a strategic deployment of information, it

was also an emotional protective device.  The men were not accustomed

to express their feelings directly, perhaps, in many cases, not even to

themselves.  Another female middle manager described,

"Men project a person who goes through a lot of
motions and getting a lot of work done without
revealing any affect about it.  I can't tell
what they feel about things and they probably
don't know how they feel about it."

Hence, competition was partly manifested as a front of self-confidence

and independence.  It was the structure that carried the manager's

interests as they were perceived from his position in the hierarchical

division of labor. Competition was a tension both within the individual
and between individuals. The tension within the individual was comprised of contrary impulses of self-interest and fear; the former
leading to aggressive action and the latter leading to obedient action.
When the self-interest impulse was strong in the individuals of a
group, then a tension arose between the individuals because scarcity
of rewards meant there would necessarily be losers. These psychological and sociological tensions, which resulted in individual attempts
to position themselves, depending on the individual, to maximize his
self-interest, minimize fear, or some balance of the two, were stoical-
ly suppressed from their direct expression. Self-interest was publically expressable up to a point, but fear was not. After years of
suppression of the tensions many managers had forgotten they were
there.

But they were there and their existence influenced the quality of
openness that was maintained throughout upper management. It was a most
striking fact that, even though regular salaries were publically
announced, bonuses were kept secret. Thus, if one got a bonus for a
superior contribution to company goals no one but the one who received
it knew about the bonus. This particular aspect of the bonus process
was never considered unusual. The decision on who on the AVP level
got "merit money" was made by the officers. A VP described that meeting,

> "It's an all-day meeting. Very heated and indepth.
> Everyone quizzes the guy backing someone on every-
> thing. If the guy comes in there ill-prepared, he
> soon looks like an ass himself. The human
> resources VP tells the other officers to pick ten
> AVPs, we're going to give it to six. The six who
> get it are going to be on everyone's list. There
> is a propensity to take care of their own."

An AVP responded to the process,

> "This plan has caused disgruntlement. A handful
> of dollars go to a handful of people, hard to
> administer them fairly. A lot of nasty remarks
> made about the nasty nine who get merit pay from
> total AVPs. The group appraisal process we have
> to decide who gets it is highly unfair. VP
> Bingham was there and hardly said a word. Some
> AVPs say this is the worst decision of the year."

Another AVP thought "nine" received merit money in 1980; another said the same ones as got it in 1979 got it in 1980. Therefore, the AVPs did not know who got it, or even how many were rewarded. I asked one of the ones who did get a bonus about it and he immediately replied he had never told anyone about it before. I asked another AVP who received a bonus what his contribution was to receive the largest bonus, but he would not discuss it. He later called the VP human resources and complained about my question. I was called in and told "you made a boo-boo with Breecher by telling him how much money he made." Open discussion of competition was taboo. At this company there was competition, but there was not an open acknowledgement of it.

The basis for cooperation, then, was a field of contrasting social and cultural patterns. Cooperative effort was shaped by a hierarchical division of labor which allotted each individual a view of the whole process and a view of his own interests within this process according to his position. On the AVP level of the hierarchy, the cooperative process was further influenced by common attachments to the public service idea, common personal needs such as desires for occupational security and stability, and similar social backgrounds and career expectations. On the other hand, however, these positive influences were disrupted by uncooperative influences. The most important of which was competition based on self-interest. On any particular issue self-interest manifested itself as tugs and pulls on the formulating of action based on group interest; that is, self-interest necessarily meant conflict was inherent in the cooperative process. And at this company conflict was not openly discussed. Thus, the cooperative process based on common purpose was problematic. The integration of these influences was the quality of cooperation which affected how the tasks were approached and how the cooperative effort was organized.

III. A Formal Structure for Cooperation

The way groups resolve conflicts and organize to meet collective goals is the process of cooperation. But the manner in which conflicts are framed and individual relations constructed is problematic in itself. In this section we will describe the interaction of managers in a formal committee. We will find that the issue of cooperation is avoided during this committee's meetings and that at this company conflict resolution is primarily pushed into the informal system of action.[6] Our analysis of this formal committee will bring us to understand why decision making and cooperation are done informally and where we should begin an analysis of the informal cooperative system.

The committee that will be the object of focus is the Corporate Planning Council (CPC). The CPC had fifteen members, all of which were staff AVPs (one division head was the secretary). The fact that the CPC was comprised of all staff and the fact that the company operations were primarily oriented towards the line, meant that this committee was not designed for immediate action. Even though many of the AVPs on the CPC had important jobs, only one of the CPC members was in the group of six that had received bonuses for their contribution to company goals in 1980. The CPC was a staff committee and staff was secondary. One might think that since the company was in a time of radical change, the staff managers would take on additional importance in order to plan for the change in operations; but as was shown in the previous chapter, the CEO did not allow much delegation of authority and what authority he did delegate, ambiguously, went to the line.

Staff was, in most areas, removed from the action. This was the general context for when the CPC was observed in 1981.

Before continuing with the analysis, it will be useful to provide a short history of the origins of the CPC. In 1960 the corporation was reorganized into a multi-functional line with a decentralized staff. This meant that a general operations manager (GOM) was assigned to each of the company's four areas with responsibility over plant, traffic, and commercial divisions; and also within each area was the appropriate staff personnel (e.g. engineering, accounting, human resources). In 1974 another reorganization resulted with the same multi-functional line, but a centralized staff. This took the staff out of the areas and put them into the headquarters building.

Also, during this period (1960 to 1974) there was a drive toward mechanization. This drive, no doubt, was primarily responsible for the changes in organizational structure. The GOM position was designed to enable an AVP to manage multiple functions and the central staff was a response to the forced centralization that comes along with mechanization. Hence, in 1974 there were staff AVPs who were responsible for disciplines on a statewide basis; and not only did they have more people to be concerned about, but also their concerns seemed more often than not to cut across other AVP disciplines. For example, the mechanization brought engineering into more contact with plant and traffic, or operations into more contact with regulation. The result was a need for a corporate policy committee. The CPC was set up for this purpose. This group was supposed to look at a variety of things that were being done and needed to be done across disciplines. The idea

was to have a formal group that would explicitly work on the new problem
of interdisciplinary action and effect policy for the business in this
regard. They were supposed to effect policy by making decisions and
then, as a group, recommend these decisions to the officers.

The CPC was set up, but the decision making never happened. An
accounting AVP described,

> "The CPC is not a practical decision making forum,
> it's an information forum. It makes no decisions.
> We lack a decision making process in the whole
> company. We don't have any authority. We assume
> that decisions are made by expenditures approval."

This AVP believed that the CPC was not making decisions because they
were not able to make decisions without authority. But they were not
even recommending decisions. His belief about this was that they did
not think that this was their job because this job was taken care of
when the officers decided who got how much money. Thus, even though it
was formally stated that this was a policy formulating committee, there
was a tendency not to believe it from the start. Another accounting
AVP added,

> "CEO Hill gave us authority to begin with [1974]
> but we immediately regrouped and changed the
> purpose. Originally a VP was supposed to come to
> the meetings, but this did not last long and when
> he did come it was symbolism."

There was no doubt that the committee shaped itself to avoid decisions.
This same AVP went on,

> "In the CPC Charter it states there should be a
> rotating chairmanship. This has not happened be-
> cause they don't want this to be a decision body."

The CPC had evolved into a "good information pool," "an excellent forum
for communications," "information sharing forum," "good way for infor-

mation trading," "informationally valuable," etc.; but not, as a regulation AVP said, to do what it was supposed to do:

> "to make formal recommendations to the officer
> group for actions and programs--a live on-going
> part of the decision process."

It was quite confusing to an observer to watch high ranking, experienced managers with considerable problems facing each one and the group as a whole, come together on a monthly basis to find out something that a five minute telephone call would achieve. I sat through three of these three hour meetings. They indeed were nothing more than presentations of "information." Much of which was technical and detailed to the point of it being hard to imagine what the details of one organization could offer to another. There was little discussion and certainly no decision making.

To the question why go to the CPC meetings, one AVP responded, "The minutes are published." Even though no other managers gave this reason, it seemed to have some validity. Before going to the April CPC meeting, I read the minutes of the March CPC meeting thinking it would help me understand the discussion. In the March CPC minutes there was a list of nine subcommittees that were formed with three to five CPC managers on each committee; some managers were on several committees. These committees were formed, the minutes said, to study problems facing the company. At the April CPC meeting the subcommittees were not mentioned. Indeed, as I checked with the CPC members' secretaries thoughout the summer and into the fall, there was no evidence that the subcommittees ever met. The secretaries had never even heard of them. Even though the minutes had discussed these subcommittees at length,

their existence was confined to that apparent discussion of them.
Hence, the CPC went through the motions but not the follow through.
AVPs attended because they were supposed to attend, and they did what
they thought they were supposed to do: Do nothing but appear to be
doing something.

The AVPs, however, could not openly acknowledge that they were
consciously doing very little if anything. This tension between formal
dictates and informal reality led to positioning as to whose fault it
was. In this case, the blame was laid on the officers. An AVP explained,

> "The officer group and Humler never gave directions
> for this group, no endorsement."

An engineering AVP added,

> "The CPC is directed by the CPC Steering Committee--
> CEO, VP Accountant, VP Regulation. They hold up the
> CPC goals."

A third AVP said, "We don't get feedback from the officers on the CPC."
But did they really want any feedback? All they had to do was ask
the officers to discuss the CPC's unresolved issues, but as an AVP told,
"We have never done this in five years." Thus we start to see the true
context of the CPC. The CPC was given no authority, it took no
initiatives, yet it continued, and the reason it continued was because
a CEO started it. It would take nothing less than a CEO to stop it.
Nobody was "going to stick out their neck." An AVP remarked,

> "The first setback for the CPC was when VP Geltner
> came to the meetings. Everyone backed off to wait
> for him to lead."

Since the CPC members were not told what to do, they did nothing.
Actual decision making was seldom done in groups because authority was

primarily personal, not legal. The CPC did nothing because they were given nothing to do and this was accepted by both the CPC members and the officers.

We saw in the previous chapter that a coalition of AVPs put together the profit committee. This was done outside of the jurisdiction of the CPC and the creator of the profit ideas was a non-CPC member. An AVP remarked,

> "A subcommittee of the CPC could have done what the profit committee is doing. We should have been the ones that saw this need. No one on the CPC had the foresight to see the gap in our planning."

This was remarkable because the profit committee was eventually comprised of managers that were almost all on the CPC, but no formal relation was established between the two. An AVP, trying to explain why a new committee was formed, said,

> "CPC members' attitudes are sit back and wait to see what your role is. Bell employees are very receptive and prone to orders. Team success sense is high at Bell. We're all here to get a job done. Nothing is too much to get the job done."

Well, nothing is too much to get the job done except initiative. It was unanimous during the interviews that the CPC was not functioning correctly and that it was a disappointment to all its members. But nobody did anything about it. One AVP said he told the CEO, but that the CEO "did not want to put the CPC and its chairman out of business." The CPC was probably started the same way the profit committee was started in 1981: A problem was formulated, someone came up with an idea, and it was implemented. The problem is that even after the initial problem goes away or the committee starts to drift away from its assignment, the committee remains. The committee does not adapt and is allowed to remain becuase it does no harm and it is easier to promote a new committee, raising someone's status and power than it is to terminate one, lowering someone's status and power.

The CPC continued to meet, so the members tried to make it as painless as possible. It was held out of town (several managers claimed this was why they went:  to avoid paying city payroll taxes for the day) and it was relaxing. My notes of the meetings show one manager spending several hours scraping the tape of his glass case; at another meeting the lights were turned out for a short public relations movie and the situation that arose was remarkably similar to a grade school movie when the teacher leaves the room; yet at another meeting an individual threw a paper ball over his shoulder to the waste basket but missed, another manager picked up the paper ball and handed it back for the manager to try again.

Also, there was an air of importance about the meetings because they were held in a high security building belonging to the parent company; it was a change from the routine and gave a feeling of superior status. In this sense, the CPC was a ritual:  It expressed to the staff AVPs their membership in a larger organization and the status they gained from such a membership. And in a time of radical change where their status and power had been lowered, this ritual played an important role.

Hence, the only positive functions of the CPC were informational and ritualistic. A division head explained,

> "It's the kind of business we're in, touch all
> bases, no bottom line. The top sixty managers

> got to the top in a monopoly environment. They
> didn't want to be in a rat race. This is a
> comfortable place to work."

There is no doubt that the CPC gave one the impression that things were comfortable. And there was also no doubt that most monopoly managers waited for directives rather than pursue their own initiatives. But no matter how protected the environment and no matter how much an order-follower a manager was, he still, at least part of the time, had to get involved with other individuals in other suborganizations with other interests and somehow take part in a cooperative effort. That we did not find the ground for this cooperative effort in these formal meetings means we must look elsewhere.

Before leaving our discussion of the CPC, however, we can glean some hints as to the nature of cooperation at this company. We saw that the most important committee on the AVP level over the last seven years had quickly evolved itself into a sharing of information forum and little more. What was avoided was taking explicit positions on issues as a group and the group conflict that would be needed to arrive at these positions. An AVP, in reference to the dysfunctional CPC, said, "We all have other techniques to get our problems solved." So now we must look somewhere else to find these techniques. We know they will not be formal, they will not be explicit, therefore they will be done informally and in a manner that guards the manager from taking an explicit position for which he can be attacked. A VP gave a hint about how this takes place:

> "Things get done by excellent individuals. Collec-
> tively the AVPs do nothing. If three are there, it
> won't work. It will be done by two, two, two."

IV.  Informal Processes to Effect Cooperation

Every manager had multiple positive relationships with other
managers in the company that were based primarily on providing mutual
support and instrumental helpfulness in securing resources, information,
and political organization to accomplish individual tasks.  We will
call these multiple positive relationships "networks."  Similar to the
telephone networks that cross and recross the country, making it possible to communicate between just about any two points, these organizational networks were vast in their comprehensiveness and efficient in
their ability to facilitate communication and organize resources.
There was no effective manager that worked without an extensive and
durable cluster of supportive co-workers.  Even though the relationships
had to be positive to be helpful, there were many types of positive
relationships.  Some were based on love, respect, admiration, loyalty;
others on fear, humiliation, blackmail, power; still others, the majority, on reciprocity and mutual advantage.  Some were vertical, others
horizontal.  They could be used daily, weekly, monthly, yearly, or
twice in a career.  What went on in these networks was the essence of
management.  When the buzzing of phone conversations, two manager
lunches, pre-meeting huddles, and quick passing exchanges in bathrooms,
hallways, stairways, or on the street stopped, the managers were not
working.

No manager accomplished goals alone, all managers had to be part
of an implicit team.  It could not be a formalized team, explicitness
was vulnerability, because if one's opponent knew one's strategy, he
could almost for sure foil it.  Therefore, the essence of corporate

work—in the sense of goal-seeking action—was conducted in the system of personal, usually face to face if it was important, relationships. And this system was to a large degree invisible and uncontrollable: Nobody knew another manager's complete array of relationships. Indeed, outspokenness and openness were unusual because of the need to guard one's avenues to collect and disperse information, resources and political support. A division head explained,

> "If you don't tell people what you think, they
> don't know what you think. If you don't put
> your cards on the table, you cannot be attacked."

There is much to learn by comparing management practices to a game of poker. The phrase "close to the vest" was also used (I heard it perhaps twelve to fifteen times over an eight month period). As we shall see, bluffs and strategies played their part in the quality of cooperation at the company.

But more than anything else, networks and their modes of operation were influenced by a ruling passion to compete. Competition powered the daily interaction of key managers. A division head analyzed,

> "Competition is on a day-to-day basis to make your
> organization look likes it's better, and to
> express the incompetence of other organizations.
> It's common to criticize other parts of the
> organization (sales, marketing). And there is
> always the competition for the budget."

If one was not keenly conscious of their competitive position vis-a-vis other managers, then their job was surely marginal. In the heart of the corporation, where the networks were buzzing with questions, bargains, promises, and lies, the competition was most acute. Compassion existed, but it was no doubt secondary. A second level manager described,

> "Concern for others does not exist other than
> accomplishing other people's needs. There is
> a great deal of compassion on a personal level,
> but not on a professional level in the sense that
> everyone is a competitor. You become concerned for
> others in the sense your interests intertwine with
> theirs. You must be seen as a cooperative indivi-
> dual if you expect to have cooperation from others."

This leads to what Erving Goffman has called "facework."[7] A manager
does not really care about all the managers he deals with, but if he
wants cooperation he must signal that he is willing to cooperate. And
part of cooperation is based on trust and trust assumes a degree of
compassion. Thus, the personal/professional dichotomy that this manager
has set up claims the need for a mechanism to conceal the frame switch:
facework. A division head explained,

> "Bradford is a classic example. He'll put on a
> face that you'll never find a more caring
> generous person. The other side of the coin is
> he is cut-throat. We're bred for this, chosen
> for this."

Networks are fundamentally professional, yet intense social con-
structions. They are used by the individual primarily to accomplish
his goals, but are at the same time charged with personal attachments.
None-the-less, their primary use was to get things done and take credit
for what was done. An AVP said,

> "Alliances change from time to time depending on
> subject matter and purpose. We always have
> alliances for ad hoc purposes."

This changing from time to time is encouraged by the individualistic
nature of the managers. A division head remarked,

> "Even though Dunter and Blane are good friends,
> they both talk behind each other's back.
> Rembler is also good friends with Dunter, but
> he too talks behind his back. Last year Blane
> tricked Dunter and got an important part of his

organization and his best people."

Networks--the social ground of cooperation--are fundamentally based on self-interest.

An organization cannot explicitly condone self-interest because it is antithetical to the idea of a collective effort. But they cannot survive without it. A female district head analyzed,

> "We're groomed and molded to respond to a vertical hierarchy by rewards and punishments, but to get any work done we must move out of the hierarchy. Most groups worry about their own interest, not those of other groups."

Another female district head added,

> "I will go to meetings to discuss specific issues and people will discuss issues in approximates, it's difficult to find a group of people who will lay their cards on the table, who will put all the facts out. What bothers me is that as a group, everyone is not working as a group or working towards a common goal. Why is this happening? Because people are more concerned with their own careers rather than the goals of the corporation. People place their priorities where they benefit the most out of the projects, rather than really working together. Many times there is no clearly defined goal, and the reward system is not in tune with goals."

Managers will not "lay their cards on the table" because if they do, they could be hurt. The vertical hierarchy is inflexible and slow in response because of increased risks due to explicitness. Thus networks develop to perform where the formal hierarchy discourages action. And since the fundamental characteristic of networks are their informality, they lend themselves to abuses of self-interest. But even if self-interest could be culturally changed to more of an emphasis on corporate interest, the information produced by informal networks would still encourage managers to work around the rigid dictates of the formal processes, because informal information flows will create divergent expectations and perceptions, thus precluding unitary action and opening up the avenue for personal advantage. Therefore, top management must insist on a formal, vertical hierarchy and staff this hierarchy with loyal personnel in order to remain in control. This is a major reason why we found in Chapter III that promotions were based more on personal characteristics than on managerial abilities, because this keeps the vertical hierarchy strong with trusted and dependent subordinates. Informal networks are not only a tool of top management, they are a constant threat, since information can flow away from formal power, thus redistributing power.

Thus self-interest, a cultural factor, merges with the structural peculiarities of information flows, in this American bureaucracy, to make networks center stage in management practices. At this company self-interest manifested itself in taking credit. A division head told,

> "The AVPs like to take credit for things they
> really don't do. One AVP told me when I came back
> from the parent company that he had supported my
> promotion there when he really had tried to get me
> a lateral. I've seen AVPs argue with district
> heads on who had made a decision to fix up things
> much before. Who gets credit is important.
> Recognition aspects are important. It's not
> uncommon for people to reach out and take credit.
> In a company this large, after a period of time,
> it's hard to figure out who was responsible for
> specific actions. Many times many people are
> involved. There's room to give credit to a
> number of people, but people try to take credit
> all themselves. They don't want to share. They
> want the brass ring for themselves. The brass
> ring usually goes to the implementor, not the
> conceiver of an idea."

Hence networks were used not only to accomplish tasks to get credit, but to get credit in and of itself. A district head said,

> "It happens a lot that people don't want to do
> something, but are forced to and if it turns out
> good then they say it was their idea."

That these things are common underlines what the previous division head said: The processes are so complex it is never clear who was responsible. This opens up an avenue for manipulation for the managers inclined to manipulate. One VP told me twice, laughing all the way through, that if you listen to Jones, another VP, he would tell you that the golf game [generally considered the company's worst publicity in a decade] was good and we ought to be glad it happened. That Jones would make this claim, underscores the fact that uncertainty exists everywhere and it is the habit of many successful managers to exploit it.

Within this uncertainty of responsibility reputation becomes extremely important. An individual with a poor reputation, for whatever reason, soon finds himself without "roots." A manager develops a reputation first and foremost with the other managers he works with. An AVP reported, "Most people have a circle of friends because of interrelationships of jobs." A district head added, "Informal networks tend to be made up with people you once worked with, so it sets up some communication and trust level." A division head explained,

> "Informal networks are made out of people I
> trust. They have some brilliance in some area,
> people I've worked with over the years. When I
> deal with an organization, I look for somebody
> in it I know and trust. Individuals are important."

Reputations, then, are developed through working relationships. A manager gets transferred and a good relationship left behind becomes a part of an extended network. This also, however, meant "all organizations have leaks." An AVP reported,

"There are leaks in Fenton's organization, I know
what his plans are.  I read two of those volumes
of the parent company guidelines over the weekend
even though I was not allowed to have copies.  I
did not want anybody knowing things I did not know."

Information was power and information was got from people, people in

other organizations.  It paid to develop a network.

Networks, however, once developed must be kept alive.  They take

work.  An AVP stated, "The grapevine, like any vine, must be cultiva-

ted, you must pay your dues."  If the transferred manager does not

maintain his potential network, it might not be available when he

needs it.  A division head remarked,

"You scratch my back, I'll scratch yours.  I do
favors and I write I.O.U.s.  Sometimes it's
spoken, sometimes you don't have to remind them.
If you don't remind them, these are the best."

A network is a socially alive process.  If one is not the network type

(for example the proverbial engineer who only wants to know the "facts"),

then his network will be weak and not responsive.  It is like a savings

account--the more you put in the more you can expect to get out.  And

similar to putting money in a bank, it would not be advisable to invest

support and information in a manager who was reputed to not return the

service.

There are other rules for who gets included in an individual's

network.  They are almost all on one's peer level.  The relationship

from the subordinate to the superior is clouded with implications of

formal power.  There are still these kinds of network type relations,

but they are fewer, since the mutual advantage relationship is not

consistently available.  It is harder to develop a mutual sense of trust, because it is always apparent that the superior could be of more assistance or could coerce the individual into cooperation if he would not cooperate freely. Also, it is difficult to be on a relaxed, friendly basis with subordinates. A marketing AVP told,

> "There are two company people that my wife and I
> are friendly with socially, but interesting enough
> I have never worked for them nor they for me. They
> are both below my level. My rank has not effected
> the relationship. One is my hunting and fishing
> buddy. We also get together socially family wise.
> We both started together on the same day and have
> been friends since. It would be very awkward if we
> ever got together in a boss/subordinate relation-
> ship."

Seldom do bosses go to lunch with subordinates in a non-business context. One AVP went as far as to say, "It is uncomfortable to be with people you make more money than inside the company." This gives a view of the intensity of interpersonal competition between managers. It is ironic that competition both stimulates network development and limits it.

Furthermore, networks are affected by broader cultural norms. If it is not encouraged to be seen with blacks or women at lunch, then it becomes difficult for blacks and women to fully develop their networks. Minorities at this company are handicapped in this regard.

Thus networks determine to a great degree the flow of information in this organization. And the flow of information, who had it, deter-mined who could effectively make decisions and take actions. Hence, once again we arrive at the necessity of a "core" group, since only certain managers would be able to gather the needed information to effectively change any set of circumstances. These were the managers that directed the corporation. They were socially acceptable, interpersonally talented, and had the energy and ambition to mold a plan of action and get others involved. A division head described what a manager had to do to "get things done":

> "Get your ducks lined up before you start, it's better than starting out cold. Knowing who makes decisions and knowing the agendas of people you need and who's receptive to ideas and know when timing of an idea is best; knowing something for their needs, what they get out of it. Better have a network to gather all this information, have your oars out there, gather them in; and give them what they need and what you want. If you want a recommendation accepted, you develop a book on a person, their agenda, their past decisions."

Another division head described how "some people are good at getting things done."

> "Decide what you want to happen, many times we just say we're too big, we'll just go on momentum. The inertia and size and split responsibility of functions means you'll have to get many people involved. So many of our processes are carved in stone with the parent company, a lot of people don't even get started. You still have to have enthusiasm. Interpersonal relations—you have to find out who other key people are and gain their support by demonstrating that there is something for them, their organization, or the corporation. You must go to various parties, make contacts, lay ground-work. If you find these things, they tend to pick up momentum of their own. A good idea that is seen as helping people and lets them share in benefits will gather momentum. These other people will push it along and take credit."

Networks were used to gather information which was used by an individual to organize a group of individuals to pursue a common purpose to accomplish personal and organizational goals.

Much of the time the obstacles against cooperation were ignorance or laziness, not conflicts of interests. Of course, we could call laziness or ignorance interests, and then they would be in conflict

with ambitious managers. In these cases the formal organization would
be used as a defense against the momentum to change that was being
created informally. Ultimately, any change would have to eventually
get formal sanctioning. The two social structures would be in a tension
until the network idea was accepted or until it was formally ruled out
as an option. A division head remarked about the MBO system in this
regard,

> "MBO can be a protective umbrella. MBO can stop
> innovation by just repeating old objectives. Many
> people talk about changing objectives, but most
> people don't do it."

Thus, in many instances formal processes are opposed to informal ones;
in fact the informal ones were created to safely test alternatives to
the formal procedures.

The tension between the formal and informal systems is a key
component in the quality of cooperation at this company. We have seen
that an "important" formal structure, the CPC, was of little use for
the cooperative effort. Then, in this section we saw that the primary
field of cooperation was constructed from informal relationships. It
was seen that protecting one's plans of action and one's self was the
reason for the emphasis on informal networks. Since total time spent
in meetings can indicate roughly the rate of change and the degree of
interaction between formal and informal systems,[8] it can be concluded
that the CPC was an important "information forum" because most decisions
were being made informally and were then in need of dissemination.
When the informal system gets out of harmony with the formal, that is
when informal decisions are not quickly integrated into the formal
process, meetings must be used as a supplementary connecting mechanism.

This is further evidence that the quality of cooperation at this company was considerably influenced by a fear of blame or sabotage (i.e. conflict), because the informal system of action dominated the decision process. It was just as important to guard one's reputation as it was to advance it, and both of these were done under the cover of trusted relationships. Thus, networks were the most important structure for cooperation because they were the first place a manager went to begin a change, and because it was the place he went when he was planning his most important actions.

**V.** <u>Conflict in Cooperation: Notes on the Transfer of the Phone Stores</u>

Early in July, I arrived at the "officers conference room" on the top floor of the headquarters building for the "Phone Stores Meeting," about five minutes before the meeting was supposed to start. I had been told by both line and staff AVPs that the other group was trying to "pull a fast one" and that this meeting was set up to settle the matter. Also, during an earlier meeting that day I had over heard a VP tell his AVP that the "phone stores meeting is going to be rowdy." In general I had not observed any open conflict at this company during the preceeding four months and was quite interested to see just how this conflict was going to be handled by the conflicting parties. I took my seat off to the side and began to watch the AVPs and VPs come in. Seven AVPs, three VPs, and two division heads were present. About a minute before the meeting was scheduled to start, the staff VP who had called the meeting whispered into the ear of his AVP, "are you going to kick it off."

"Kick it off" was a reference to football, and that's just how these managers saw themselves and the situation they were in. The goal was not to score points, but to control resources and gain the status and security this control brought. They were all aware that two teams were present, line and staff, and that each team's goals conflicted with the other team. Even though the outcome was uncertain, they did know that there would be a winner and a loser at the end of the meeting, because one team would gain and the other lose in terms of the present control over the phone stores. If nothing changed, then that meant the line had won, because this meeting had been called by staff to take control of the responsibility for the phone stores from the line.

This type of uncertainty was the major kind of uncertainty that the monopoly managers faced. It was an uncertainty as to what other managers would do to take control over resources that someone else controlled. The monopoly manager's primary orientation on these top levels of management was towards each other, since that was where the most serious threat to one's performance and thus one's rewards came from.

The staff AVP who was about to start the meeting turned to me and said, "Something came up, would you mind stepping out for ten minutes." After being out in the hall for about eight minutes, this same AVP came out and headed for the telephone, but was caught up to and stopped by a line AVP who had followed him out of the meeting. The line AVP came out hitting the fist of his right hand into the open palm of his left hand. He said something to the staff AVP who then laughed (the line AVP did not laugh), the staff AVP turned around and headed toward the phone. He called his secretary and told her to type up a job change announcement for one of his division heads (one of the division heads at the meeting) and make it public immediately. He then turned to me and told me I could go back in.

The job change announcement was the turning point in the conflict over the phone stores. It meant that the staff had won and that they were immediately setting up an administrative unit for control of the phone stores operations. This formal action was the culmination of a process of informal work. A staff manager told about his informal preparation just for this meeting:

> "Incredibly successful meeting. I accomplished
> all my objectives with minimum pain. I expected
> a tough meeting, but I talked to all the parti-
> cipants one or two times before to know where
> they were coming from. I played to the crowd.
> My charts reflected their worries and concerns
> from my phone calls to them: 'What should I
> know? What bothers you?'"

The reason this staff manager was able to make this informal connection to reduce the conflict was because he had been a line manager
and thus was part of the networks of his old teammates, the line
managers. But, as we will see, this informal work was just the end of
a long process of informal actions that was the underpinning of this
meeting.

Upon returning to the meeting, it was obvious the climax was
already over. A red faced AVP was telling a VP, "Yeah, we do the
giving and you do the taking. After today I'm a plucked chicken."
The reason the climax had come so quickly and the shift of power so
easily was because the power trade-offs had been done informally before
the meeting. However, the fact that I was asked to leave is an indica-
tion of how cloudy the informal system is, because the staff was partly
still suspecting a counter-attack or a double-cross on the agreements
made informally. They did not want me to record an out of control
meeting. When most action is done informally, "surprises" become an
important category of interaction.

Furthermore, even though most of the line AVPs knew beforehand
that staff had a good chance of taking over the phone stores, some did
not. I asked a line AVP why his teammate with the red face was so
surprised. He replied:

> "I don't know if Briggs was covered. I don't know

if he got the pre-meeting presentation. If Jones
[the manager giving the presentation] did not cover
the rest of us, he would have gotten chopped up
more. We told Kyle [line VP] we had been covered.

Thus, Briggs' network was not up to par and he was not seen as a threat,
so the staff did not bother to "cover" him. There was no point in
alerting an opponent to one's intention if there was no advantage to it.

The meeting went on from this point for about two hours. But the
new context was clear: Staff was taking over the Phone Stores. Now
the question became more operational than political. One staff manager
gave a presentation on just how the takeover should be carried out:
The when and how of the change of control. So the interests of the
line managers, now that it was clear that they had lost control, was
to make the "cut" in a manner that did the least possible damage to
their productivity results. What I witnessed in these two hours was
argument and counterargument on technical points. A line AVP described
his view of the process:

"We think they were trying to duck part of the
phone stores' functions: repair of sets and
removal of sets. I made sure this was included
in the proposal or else they would get the stores
but we would still have to do repair and removal."

Hence, the line was down but not out. They were forced to agree to
give up the stores but were going to try to enhance their position in
the technical discussion or delay the process. A line AVP reported
that his VP whispered into his ear before he left, "Don't get tied
down to any dates." The staff, of course, had a different view of what
was going on in these two hours. A staff manager explained:

"That whole gang wanted to drag this out as long
as possible. Anything the field wants to do you
can do, but if they don't like it they will find

a million faults."

Thus, we have a picture of two coalitions locked in formal conflict over just how the "cut" of responsibilities for the phone stores should be made.

But why did the line lose the overall fight in those first ten minutes (or in the informal system earlier that week)? An AVP reported that it was an AT&T directive that the stores had to be "straight-lined" and only the staff could do this. But this directive had come down three years ago, so why was it just this July that the staff had the power to force the line into giving up control? The answer to this question is a complex one.

A line AVP told his view:

> "Snyder snuck a clause in the Transition Team report suggesting that phone center stores go over to the FSS [part of a new organization controlled by what was then called staff]. Breecher then on the golf course with Lumley [CEO], somehow talked Lumley into signing it. Lumley thought the whole team—Simmons and Kyle —had approved it [line VPs], which was not the case. Mends [SVP] then also signed it, probably before Lumley; Mends signed it without reading it—perhaps—because he would not have signed it otherwise. Lumley was mad according to Kyle, once he realized he had been fed inaccruate information. Mends would not cancel the order once he realized it was a mistake because of embarrassment."

A staff AVP reported his side of the story in a more long-term perspective:

> "Three years ago we made a presentation for me to take over the stores. It was given to Simmons and Kyle [line VPs] and they hooted us down— asked questions we could not answer. Snyder [this AVP's boss and head of the staff coalition] has smarted over this since. The mystery shopper found the stores were poorly run. Snyder has

> pressure from AT&T to get them running correctly.
> [So what we did was:] Snyder said Mends was ready;
> Tooney [another staff AVP] said Simmons and Kyle
> were ready, so I put a draft together and to my
> amazement Shinkle [a VP] signed it, May 15. On
> May 25 Mends signed it, but no one confided in
> Simmons and Kyle or the line AVPs. The assessment
> was everyone was behind it. On May 26 Mends met
> with Simmons and Kyle and told them about it; but
> nobody understood what he was saying. On May 27
> the CEO signed it. I called the line AVPs to tell
> them and Tooney called Simmons—Simmons [the center
> of the line coalition] was livid, he was abusive.
> Simmons then called me, he was abusive, 'you mother
> fucker.' They don't want to give us the stores,
> because of the way we did it. We shoved it up
> their ass. We had little choice but to do it
> this way, because they would have never agreed
> to it."

It is difficult to say whether the CEO and the SVP were duped into signing or whether they faced increasing pressure from AT&T. Nonetheless, the important point is that they were either duped by distorted information or knew very well what was going on and still had to go through the back roads of the organizations to get it done. The point is that to get it done it had to be done in secret or the opponents of the plan would have been able to stop it.

Thus, the reason the staff was able to pull it off in July of 1981, whereas they were not able three years earlier was: one, they proceeded through their networks in secret, thus by the time the conflict broke into the open their coalition was backed by the SVP and CEO; and two, the SVP and CEO were in a more neutral position in general because of the reorganization plans at AT&T. The meeting that I attended was like the tip of the iceberg: It was the formal part of the process and had little to do with the heart of the decision process on this issue. Still though, staff was not sure of their position until the secretary typed up that job change announcement for the staff division head and made it public to the company that he was taking charge of the phone stores operations. Thus, the relationship of the informal process to the formal one is intimate to say the least. It did not become formal until a public announcement had been made, because a reversal after this point would cause the signing authority public embarrassment. And embarrassment affects reputation and reputation effects power and status.

From this case we can see that the informal process and the formal process do not run one after the other, but at times are inside of each other. Thus, situations can be vastly different depending on the degree of each process involved and just how the two processes are in relation to each other in any situation. It is the task of the organizational researcher to untangle the two meaning systems bound up in a particular action. He can be assisted by the concepts of networks and coalitions. Networks are totally informal and partially secret, while coalitions consist of mostly formal action. We have just seen that the staff coalition used its networks to gather information and influence the positions of higher authorities on the phone store issue. Their coalition was formed informally, but once the conflict became public, the coalition evolved into a formal structure. Their networks were always working informally because they were used only in one-on-one situations. Thus, networks are the primary informal component of coalitions which are the primary formal structure for the field of conflict resolution.

The relationship between the concept of network and the concept of coalition helps explain more about the relationship of formal process to informal process. Networks are informal and tell us that informal processes are fundamentally limited to two individuals where a sense of trust, rightly or wrongly, is maintained. Thus, informal processes cannot be spontaneous unless the individuals involved know each other and have developed a "book" on each other. Without this the means to conduct informal interactions would be absent, since it would be impossible to contextualize what the other individual's actions and information really meant. So we would expect to find vast informal networks in organizations where individuals have known each other over a long period of time. And at this company, filled with single career managers, that is just what we did find.

Coalitions are fundamentally formed formally because they are needed for open conflict against previously established formal obstacles, whether they be rules or status quo coalitions: 'You can't beat something with nothing.' Also, coalitions must be formal for deception; that is, a coalition many times is a front, that is why even though the coalitions were known at the phone stores meeting, the outcome still was not known because the coalition could change shape once all the hidden implications of the network relations manifested themselves.

Networks are more fundamental than coalitions in established organizations (as are informal processes to formal processes) because relationships become so complex, informationally speaking, that the possibility for coalitions and strategies becomes nearly infinite. In an organization that is young or one that has a constant flow through of new personnel, the networks would be limited, coalitions more numerous and stable, and the capacity for secret relationships more inhibited by the lack of knowledge about and trust in other managers.

These theoretical points about coalitions and networks are also limited by the culture within which they must work. The phone stores drama was fundamentally propelled by a cultural category of self-interest. As the cultural influence on this central catetory varies, so will the relationship between formal and informal processes as they are found in any organization.

V.   Conclusion

We have found two major motivations in the cooperative process:
Motivation based on public service and motivation based on self-
interest. The motivation for public service was explicitly cultivated
at this company because it enhanced the company's ability to maintain
its use to the tax payers. Also, it was implicitly desired by many
managers because they had come to the company to be able to belong to
a community oriented organization.

Powerful managers, however, were less interested in community
service and more interested in personal accomplishment. And it was
these managers that were at the heart of the cooperative process. But
even these managers were forced to at least outwardly work toward
community interests, such was the power of the community service theme
in the culture as a whole.

Nonetheless, power in the hands of self-interested individuals was
the primary influence on the shape of the cooperative process. These
individuals formed into coalitions to effect change that was advantageous to their ambitions. It was found that coalitions were mostly
formal structures that served as the means for conflict resolution.
Coalition members all had networks which were used informally to gather
information and support for their coalition.

Networks and coalitions were seen as the two concepts that described the actions taking place informally and formally. Because the
members of coalitions also had networks and were usually involved in
both at the same time, the cooperative process was characterized as a
field of action which had both a formal and informal element. It is

nearly certain that no action can be considered informal or formal, but must have both dimensions of meaning attributed to it.

Networks and thus informal processes were found to be the primary level of action at this company. This was explained by the intimate awareness that the participants had of each other because of the many years of working together. At this company the cooperative process was maintained by formal actions and formal structures, but the dynamic movement of these actions and structures was fundamentally powered by informal action and meaning.

Furthermore, all cooperative processes were limited by cultural norms that regulated the types of relationships that could be formed. Categories of a racial, sexual, and behavioral nature were in existence that were apriori instruments to control which individiuals were accepted into networks to begin with. Thus, these apriori categories and the categories of self-interest and public service structured the context of meaning in which all cooperative action took place.

## ENDNOTES

1. Some students of social groups have found that conflict is integral to social organization. Simmel stated, "A certain amount of discord, inner divergence and outer controversy, is organically tied up with the very elements that ultimately hold the group together; it cannot be separated from the unity of the sociological structure." Georg Simmel, Conflict. New York: The Free Press, 1955, p. 17-18.

2. The First 100. Company publication. September, 1979. Some of these corporately honored acts resulted in the death of the employee who was credited with heroism.

3. ibid.

4. "...if the participants feel that their relationships are tenuous, they will avoid conflict, fearing that it might endanger the continuance of the relation." Lewis A. Coser, The Functions of Social Conflict. New York: The Free Press, 1956. p. 85.

5. This common orientation towards women of most male managers appears to rest on the belief that women are seen as wives and mothers easier than as managers. Kanter writes, "Women have been assumed not to have the dedication of men to their work, or they have been seen to have conflicting loyalties, competing pulls from their other relationships." Rosabeth Moss Kanter, Men and Women of the Corporation. New York: Basic Books, 1977. p. 66.

6. There is not a fine distinction between formal and informal action, but a hazy one. Dalton figured, "Accepting the terms 'formal' and 'informal' as helpful labels for the two poles, we saw that they are held together by meetings, unofficially ordered or granted departures from the formal, transitional roles, prefigured justifications, the role of the "two-way funnel" [using go-betweens to facilitate communication], and the eventual formalizing of sound or inescapable practices that may have earlier been taboo. ...however purely evasive or organizationally superfluous the informal may be, the formal restrains it in at least three ways. First, the formal largely orders the direction the informal takes. Second, it consequently shapes the character of defenses created by the informal. And third, whether the formal is brightly or dimly existent in the blur of contradictions, it requires overt conformity to its precepts." Melville Dalton, Men Who Manage. New York: John Wiley & Sons, Inc., 1959. p. 237.

7. Erving Goffman, Interaction Ritual. New York: Patheon Books, 1967. Goffman calls this facework a ritual that reflects moral rules that are impressed on the individual from the outside. Thus, again we see that this company culture suppresses open aggression, but encourages a covered attempt to secure one's advantage.

8. Dalton, p. 228.

Chapter V

CONCLUSION: AN ESSAY ON CULTURE IN ORGANIZATIONAL PROCESS

Culture is a cluster of symbolic forms that says something of something. Symbolic forms are used to give meaning to the objects—people, places, things, feelings—that we perceive. In the beginning was the word, the word is a symbolic form, before symbol was before the beginning. But the way we use symbols has evolved. The concept of symbol, in modern times, has become merged with the concept of allegory.[1] Today, they both represent something other than themselves. Before the seventeenth century, before the efforescence of the physical sciences, a symbol was what it represented, not something other. The physical sciences, in the west, moved the dominion of truth, for most of us, from the transcendental to the mundane. Now, instead of the symbolic order being the really real one, the mundane is the really real one. Thus, symbol has become "merely symbolic" and moved out of the main area of understanding of human life. As long as man gives meaning to his existence, however, he will use a transcendent symbolic order to structure that meaning.[2] Hence, to more fully understand the social world, we must study the symbolic dimension of it.

The study of modern organizations is no exception. Even though we have been taught to believe we are able to perceive objects in and of themselves, there must be a subjective-symbolic element in every perception or cognition.[3] This symbolic element is culture. Now it is not possible for this symbolic element to wholly originate in social units as young and as small as organizations, because these social units always come into being within larger contexts and are comprised of individuals with previous cultural impressions. Thus, the ideational structure of the cultural aspects of organizations can never wholly be a system with independent semantic integrity. Its cultural structure is mostly dependent on ideational elements that originated and are fundamentally maintained external to the corporate existence.

There is, however, an element of culture that always originates within the organization, because only in particular actions does culture exist. William Blake put it thus:

> "If the Spectator could Enter into these Images in
> his Imagination, approaching them on the Fiery
> Chariot of his Contemplative Thought, if he could
> Enter into Noah's Rainbow or into his bosom, or
> could make a Friend & Companion of one of these
> Images of wonder, which always intreats him to
> leave mortal things (as he must know), then would
> he arise from his Grave, then he would meet the
> Lord in the Air & then he would be happy.  General
> Knowledge is Remote Knowledge; it is in Particulars
> that Wisdom consists..."[4]

Indeed, "it is in Particulars that Wisdom consists." This means that even though the ideational aspect of culture usually originates in the historical context external to the organization, the particular social structure of the organization and the particular individuals involved in that organization come together to create or recreate the ideational aspect anew when they act in a particular situation.

Thus, the cultural aspects of organizations are a tension between the broader historical context where from the original ideational structure mostly comes and the recreation of that structure in the forging of particular actions (which is existence).  Cultural aspects of organizations can never be wholly reduced to the organization as an independent creator of its own truth, because there usually is no ideational element that was not already alive in the actions of other individuals in the history of the broader culture of which that organization is a part; and even if the organization creates a new ideational category, it still must be composed from elements in the broader culture. Thus, only a part of the categories in use by organizational participants can we describe as "organizational culture." And this part of the cultural aspect of organizations which we will call organizational culture will always at least be a reference to the uniqueness of a particular action in a local setting, the lowest level of general ideas (culture). Hence, the concept of organizational culture is a valid concept as long as it: one, expresses its dependence on the broader historical context; two, recognizes that it will usually only account for the least general level of culture that influences the organization's members. Understanding the cultural aspects of organizations must always include an understanding of the broader regional and national cultures of which they are a part. However, as we will show in this organization, some organizations do have original cultural categories, thus having two levels of organizational categories, one based on the uniqueness of that locality and the other based on the creation and maintenance of an original idea through its history, within their organizational cultures.

In this study an additional culture and social structure had to be accounted for. It was the broader telephone system of which this utility was a part. Thus, to accurately describe the aspects of this corporate culture that we were concerned with, we had to incorporate social structural and cultural factors of American attitudes to author-

ity, demographic facts about regional religions, customs, and traditions, the structure of the broader telephone system, and lastly the
particular actions of individuals within the organization. It is only
through the service of a hierarchy of generalizations that the complexity of the cultural aspects of organizations can be interpreted, and
within this hierarchy the "organizational culture" specified.

In this particular study our primary objective was to describe the
cultural aspects of interpersonal relations as they influenced the
career development and cooperative processes. It was our central
hypothesis that the categories of interpersonal relations were the
core categories of organizational culture. In this organization it
was found that the heart of the career development process was the
manager's relation to authority. A manager, to gain responsibility
and power, had to win the backing of higher authorities who would then
raise his rank in the formal hierarchy. This was mostly done through
personal ties which were in turn mostly informal. And this informal
system of personal ties was structured by an idea of authority that
was based on the obedience to and respect for individuals in central
positions of power: Institutional charismatic authority.

The distribution of institutional charismatic authority was controlled by rules for the forming of personal ties which was the only
means to get support for promotion. Apriori categories of a sexual,
religious, and ethnic nature were found that limited the span of acceptable relationships. Furthermore, categories for appropriate behavior
that influenced subordinates to adapt to the managerial styles of the
superior as they manifested themselves in the superior's actions to

achieve his goals and to adapt in a deference signalling manner to the personal-emotional needs of the superior were the central categories for career advancement. Deference signalling abilities were the most important because the competition between subordinates meant an individual had to do more than accomplish his goals to get recognition. This was especially true in this study of monopoly management because the crucial element in displaying managerial skill, dealing with uncertainty, was much less a factor than in marketplace management, because of the lowering of the cost of information and the extension of the time period for production due to monopoly conditions of trade. Hence, in monopoly management the interpersonal factor gained additional importance over the social structural factor.

Within the cultural categories of interpersonal relations for career development, the central category was conformity. The ability to conform to the managerial style of one's continually changing superiors and to conform to the appropriate obedience position as expressed through deference signalling was the heart of the category of conformity. This category and the apriori categories for restriction of the promotable population resulted in a hierarchy that was able to maintain high degrees of control, but able to show little adaptability. However, control was what was needed, not adaptability, for the period after World War II and into the 1970s, before the monopoly protective shield started to crumble. This was true because revenues came from regulators and corporate image was the key to winning favorable revenue levels from the regulators. And corporate image was maintained through managerial control.

Thus, we see culture is context. Context is the structure of meaning in which we interpret action or potential action and respond to it with our own actions. The role of culture in the career development process is one of limiting and defining any situation through the use of categories that are used by the individual's cognition of them. When a black man sees that there has never been a black AVP or VP at this utility in one hundred and three years, he does not attribute this to chance, but to the way of life or ethos of the group in control. There are certain ways things are always done and there are certain ways things are never done, and it is the cultural tendencies that are primarily responsible for this.

That an ambitious young manager must start to cultivate a particular kind of appearance and must cultivate personal ties with superiors within the limits of certain acceptable deference signalling styles is culture. Culture is not a general rule that hovers over a group like a cloud, but is the general pattern of behavior that can be observed in the individual actions of group members.

In this study of monopoly managers we found the cultural aspect of interpersonal relations in the career development process to be based on personal ties that were structured by a belief in charismatic authority. This type of charisma was rooted in the awe-inspiring reaction to institutional power as it is represented in particular individuals. It was not a belief in the superior quality of any individual, but only the authority of that individual as he commanded it through his office. It was not a belief in the rules that provide for such a structure, but only the fact that within the organization

certain individuals represent, in their body, the organizational authority to control, alter, and direct the individuals within the organization and the organization as a whole.

The structure of institutional charisma is based on a belief of
personal embodiment of organizational power and this belief is a cultural factor. Career development, on its face, is a social structural
phenomenon. But this formal picture can only be truly understood when
its dynamic or its movement is understood. And its movement can only
be understood if we can comprehend why the individuals involved act the
way they act to cause the particular form of movement that the structure
has continuously manifested. And the main principle or belief that
initiates the actions of these monopoly managers is the desire to gain
or incorporate the charisma associated with office, to wear it on their
body, and the other side of this, the inseparable side, is that they
have to adapt to their superiors through deference signalling because
these superiors already have the institutional charismatic authority
which demands obedience.

Therefore, culture is context and context is the fundamental
structure of organizations, because it gives meaning to the processes
of organizations, the processes do not primarily give meaning to culture, because to be a particular process in the first place is to be
culturally recognized. And our hypothesis about the cultural aspects
of interpersonal relations being the core categories of organizational
culture is given support by our study of the career development process,
because we found the belief in institutional charisma, a cultural
form, to be at the heart of the explanation of how the career develop-

ment process is viewed by the participants in it, and thus the reason for their actions that give it its particular dynamic shape.

Let us now turn to the cultural aspects of interpersonal relations with regard to the cooperative process. We found that the cooperative process was powered by the goals of the company as a whole as they were perceived within the context of the broader socio-economic community and the goals of particular individuals as they were perceived within the context of the organization. At the origin of cooperative action were usually two self-interested individuals formulating their plans informally. This was called networking and was the central concept to understanding the cooperative process. Networks were the manager's set of informal relationships that were used to gather information and organize resources to effect change.

Network relationships were found to be positive in the sense that they were geared for mutual advantage, not sabotage. If one manager was caught causing negative results to the cooperative efforts of another manager, he was removed from the network, which meant he was no longer informally advised of the true intentions of the other manager. Thus, networks were personable in the sense that they needed a certain sense of trust between individuals to be maintained. Trust many times grew into friendship and longstanding network relations usually were thick with attachments of loyalty, dedication, affection, etc.

Sabotage or conflict, however, was still an element in the cooperative process. Once a network was activated for a certain goal, coalitions would form from the different interests managers had in relation to that goal. The conflict would be between coalitions and the networks were used to gather information and support to attempt to neutralize the opposing coalition and insure one's own goals were met. Thus, networks were mostly constructed to gain support, while coalitions were constructed for conflict. However, networks could be used to feed false or distorted information to a coalition. Some managers developed considerable skills at doing this without getting caught.

The manager's goals that stimulated networking and coalition building were always a merging of the manager's career ambitions and the organization's goals as they were defined formally. The latter were always more ambiguously defined because of their generality. This led to their being open to broad interpretations, which usually were heavily influenced by the particular interests of the manager-interpreter doing the interpreting.

However, the belief in public service was found to be a corporate goal that was very much alive in the decision making of the majority of managers. The company had trained their managers to think this way and the company, being a public utility and stressing public service, attracted managers interested in getting involved in this kind of industrial organization to satisfy their own social-emotional needs.

But at the core of the networking and the coalition building, and thus at the core of the cooperative process, were the powerful and power motivated managers. These managers were motivated by personal achievement.[5] They outwardly had to obey the cultural norm for public service, but within their networks, or more importantly within their ambitions and schemes because they ultimately were coalitions of one, they planned and strategized to advance their power and status. Hence, more than anything else, the cooperative process was directed by managers out to accomplish personal goals to advance their interests (which in this monopoly could sometimes be to avoid responsibilities and work rather than gain power and status).

Nonetheless, ambitious managers were usually out for power and status and it was this self-interest category that was central to the forming of cooperative action. But the self-interest category was limited because the capacity to build networks and coalitions was limited by cultural norms that preferred certain sexual, racial, and ethnic types over others. Thus, the most important and active networks were only within a certain population of the organization as a whole. The remainder of the organization, the majority, were brought into the cooperative process at later periods of the process, usually a period when the conflict was mostly finished and a formal implementation strategy had been devised. Thus, the self-interest category was most to be found in the centers of power where networks and coalitions could most easily be developed.

The self-interest category is a central category in American culture.[6] Since the majority of American managers work in competitive industries and historically this was even more so, it is not surprising to find self-interest at the heart of the cooperative process at this company. What is surprising is to find the corporate cultural category of "public service" to be so important in the motivation of the managers of this study. Most of these managers were conflict averse and were more interested to belong to a "team" than to be powerful and honored.

It is a most important social structural fact to note that the

conflict averse individuals, however, were unable to control the cooperative process and that the culturally less numerous aggressive
types were in positions of active power. The overall culture of cooperation was one of control. And it was the power motivated managers
that did the controlling. Hence, it was the interrelationships between
the primarily self-interested individuals and the primarily public-
interested individuals that was at the heart of the cooperative process.
Thus, this culture of control had been a merging of the American cultural form of utilitarian-individualism[7] with a corporate cultural
belief of public service (i.e., team-work, dedication, and stability),
which resulted in a public spirited corporation that was dominated by
self-interested individuals.

From this we can learn that corporate cultures can in fact develop
original cultural categories beyond the categories evolving from the
uniqueness of the local situation. Even though we must temper this
conclusion with the fact that this telephone utility was a member of a
larger telephone system with close to one million employees and with a
centralized management authority that had a great influence on the
basic structure and practices of this particular organization. Regardless, the fact that a unique cultural category was in existence (self-
interest tempered with motivations for community interest and team-work)
points toward the conclusion that complex organizational cultures do
exist (since the telephone system is an organization).

Now, previously we stated a corporate culture was limited in its
ability to create its own truth (category), so how can we explain the
discovery of a cultural category unique to this telephone system as

found in this organization? We must locate a creator and a semantic domain that he created. And it just so happens that we do not have far to search. In the telephone system history an originator of the idea of service did exist and he has been turned into a symbol of service that successive generations of telephone employees interpreted to build a unique cultural category that is central to their understanding of themselves and their work.

The originator of the idea of a telephone system based on universal service and organized as a monopoly was Theodore N. Vail. Vail as creator of an idea has been turned into a symbol of service which has been the central category of the company ethos for a hundred years. This symbol signifies honesty, dedication, and selflessness. Implicitly it is the original power that expresses the "service" meaning that attracted the individuals interested in working for a company that explicitly advertized itself as a part of the community, loyal to the community. Here is a quote from a company publication:

> "Theodore Vail sounded the keynote for corporate
> candor when he said, 'If we don't tell the truth
> about ourselves, someone else will.' The Company
> has heeded Vail's advice, using every means avail-
> able to tell the company's story, from press
> releases, films, lectures and displays, to an
> aggressive program in schools and colleges and
> other person-to-person programs dating back
> many years."[8]

This article goes on to discuss the company's practice of "open house" in 1928, or "Open House Program" in 1937, or "today's Share Owner Open Houses." The Vail idea has been expanded and solidified into a symbol of service that is the formal face and historical ground of the company. This corporate culture had an origin and an originator. He founded it, created a symbolic fixed point from which a culture could grow. And grow it did. It was, economically speaking, thought to be a good idea, so some individuals got involved primarily to make money, others got involved primarily for the meaning the work had for them, still others for both reasons. And a corporate culture came into existence with economic value (self-interest) and public service (perhaps a secularized form of Christianity for some) as its main cultural categories.

And this was all signified by the symbol service, which in turn was a development of the symbolization of Vail. Many of the more sensitive managers were well aware of Vail and his role in shaping the telephone system. Vail represented the community as a whole. One big family. One was not coming to work for a corporation, but for an "open house." The boundaries were down, so the company symbolized a conflict-free work life, because boundaries mean conflict. Boundaries must be enforced. At the telephone company one was working for the community, one was in the community house, one was appreciated and accepted because he was not out to take from one bounded area for his own bounded area, but instead was making a fuller commitment to the one community. Fulfillment was in belonging to unity and the telephone system symbolized unity because of monopoly, because of public service, and because the originator Vail was seen as the father of "universal service."

The awards discussed in section two of the cooperation chapter for "heroic acts of service" were the "Vail Awards." Thus, we see that the telephone system had its own semantic domain (cultural category), since it had an original idea that was historically developed through successive generations, and since it was socially maintained by the group as a whole through the patterns of their individual behavior. The semantic integrity was on the telephone system level and not the organizational level, but the telephone system was a large scale organization itself. Therefore, we could expect to find some organizational cultures with two parts to their semantic structure: one, the part found in particular action which is formed from general knowledge of the local situation; and two, any part that was created for that particular structure and developed over many generations to give it an historical integrity. This latter part, the more general part, would have a certain amount of independence from the broader historical context because of its own richness and stability, which it derived from its own historical development.

Thus, we see that the cooperative process was fundamentally a cultural phenomenon, because it was primarily influenced by meanings that shaped the patterns of behavior of the participants. Social structure played a role, but social structure at this company was seen as a means to institute "universal service" and a means for self-interested managers to achieve their goals. Both of these motivations--public service and self-interest--were culturally ingrained. Furthermore, the final actions of these managers in the cooperative effort were a merging of these two motivations, thus it was not only a cultural phenomenon that influenced these managers, but an organizational cultural phenomenon. As one retired telephone executive said: "Once a telephone man, always a telephone man."

From this study we can learn three things. One, which we have just stated, is that culture plays the primary role in organizational processes. Two, interpersonal relations are the central cultural aspects of organizational cultures as was shown in the career development and cooperative processes. Three, to study the cultural aspects of organizations is to explicate the hierarchy of generalizations that are found in the patterns of behavior of organizational members. It is the primary task of the cultural theorist to locate which level of culture is dominating in the actions of individuals in that organization; and to specify what parts of the culture are primarily internal to the organization and what parts are derived primarily from the historical context within which that organization is a part. Different organizations with different histories, different demographic compositions, different purposes, different structures, will manifest culture in different ways. Here we found the primary level of culture to be a merging of American self-interest (utilitarianism and independence) with the telephone system tradition of community service. It is only when many organizations have been interpreted in this way will we be empirically able to develop a general theory about the role of culture in organizational process.

## ENDNOTES

1. Erich Heller. The Disinherited Mind. (New York: Harcourt, Brace, Jovanovich, 1975).

2. Max Weber. Max Weber: Essays in Sociology, edited by Hans Gerth and C. Wright Mills. (New York: Oxford University Press, 1946).

3. Hans-Georg Gadamer. Philosophical Hermeneutics (Berkeley: University of California Press, 1976).

4. William Blake. "A Vision of the Last Judgement," in Blake: Complete Writings, edited by Geoffrey Keynes. (New York: Oxford University Press, 1966).

5. David C. McClelland and David H. Burnham. "Power is the great motivator," Harvard Business Review March-April, 1976, pg. 99.

6. "A note of individuals sounds through the business creed like the pitch in a Byzantine choir. We have heard it repeatedly--in the emphasis on 'self reliance,' on the importance of private business decisions, and on the dangers of collective dependence on the welfare state." Francis X. Sutton and James Tobin, The American Business Creed. (New York: Schocken Books, 1956, p. 251.)

7. Thomas C. Cochran. "Theory, Culture, and History." Unpublished paper, University of Pennsylvania 1982.

8. "The First 100 Years," Company Publication. September, 1979.

# Bibliography

Alchian, Armen A. "Competition, Monopoly and the Pursuit of Money, in Economic Forces at Work. Indianapolis: Liberty Press, 1977.

Arrow, Kenneth J. The Limits of Organization. New York: W.W. Norton and Company, 1974.

Bartlett, Randall. Economic Foundations of Political Power. New York: The Free Press, 1973.

Becker, Gary S. The Economics of Discrimination. Chicago: Chicago University Press, 1957.

Bellah, Robert N. Beyond Belief. New York: Harper and Row, Publishers, 1970.

Bernikow, Louise. "Alone: Yearning for Companionship in America," The New York Times Magazine, August 15, 1982.

Blake, William. Blake: Complete Writings. Edited by Geoffrey Keyes. New York: Oxford University Press, 1966.

Cochran, Thomas C. Business in American Life: A History. New York: McGraw-Hill Book Company, 1972.

Cochran, Thomas C. Benjamin Franklin Professor Emeritus of History, University of Pennsylvania. Personal Communication, February, 1982.

Cochran, Thomas C. "Theory, Culture and History." Unpublished paper, Radnor, Pennsylvania, 1982.

Coser, Lewis. The Functions of Social Conflict. New York: The Free Press, 1956.

Dalton, Melville. Men Who Manage. New York: Wiley, 1959.

Director, Aaron and Levi, Edward H. "Trade Regulation," Northwestern Law Review. 1956, pg. 286.

Erikson, Erik H. Childhood and Society. New York: W.W. Norton and Company, 1950.

Ferguson, C.E. and Gould, J.P. Microeconomic Theory. Homewood, Illinois: Richard D. Irwin, 1975.

Gadamer, Hans-Georg. Philosophical Hermeneutics. Berkeley: University of California Press, 1976.

Geertz, Clifford. _The Interpretation of Cultures_. New York: Basic Books, 1973.

Geertz, Clifford. "Suq: the bazaar economy in Sefrou," in _Meaning and Order in Moroccan Society_, by C. Geertz, H. Geertz, and P. Rabinow. Cambridge: Cambridge University Press, 1979.

Goffman, Erving. _Interaction Ritual_. New York: Pantheon Books, 1967.

Heidegger, Martin. _Basic Writings_. New York: Harper and Row, Publishers, 1977.

Heller, Erich. _The Disinherited Mind_. New York: Harcourt, Brace Jovanovich, 1975.

Hicks, John R. "Annual Survey of Economic Survey: The Theory of Monopoly," Econometrica, January, 1935, pg. 8.

Kanter, Rosabeth Moss. _Men and Women of the Corporation_. New York: Basic Books, 1977.

Knight, Frank H. _Risk, Uncertainty, Profit_. Chicago: University of Chicago Press, 1921.

Marschak, Jacob. "Economics of Inquiring, Communicating, Deciding," _American Economic Review Papers and Proceedings_, 58: 1-18, 1968.

McClelland, David C. and Burnham, David H. "Power is the great motivator," _Harvard Business Review_, March-April, 1976, pg. 99.

Parsons, Talcott and Shils, Edward. _Toward a General Theory of Action_. Cambridge: Harvard University Press, 1951.

Ricoeur, Paul. _The Conflict of Interpretations_. Evanston: Northwestern University Press, 1974.

Schumpeter, Joseph A. _Capitalism, Socialism, and Democracy_. New York: Harper and Row, 1942.

Shils, Edward. "Charisma, Order and Status," in _Center and Periphery: Essays in Macrosociology_. Chicago: University of Chicago Press, 1975.

Shils, Edward. "Primordial, Personal, Sacred, and Civil Ties," _British Journal of Sociology_, Vol. 8 (1957), pg. 130.

Simmel, Georg. _Conflict_. New York: The Free Press, 1955.

Sontag, Susan. "Writing Itself: On Roland Barthes," _The New Yorker_, April 26, 1982, pg. 122.

Sorokin, Pitkin. <u>Social and Cultural Dynamics</u>. 3 vols. New York: American Book Company, 1937.

Stigler, George J. "The Division of Labor is Limited by the Extent of the Market," <u>The Journal of Political Economy</u>, June 1951, pg. 185.

Stigler, George J. "The Economics of Information," <u>The Journal of Political Economy</u>, June 1961, pg. 213.

Sutton, Francis X. and Tobin, James. <u>The American Business Creed</u>. New York: Schocken Books, 1956.

Wallace, Anthony. <u>Culture and Personality</u>. New York: Random House, 1961.

Weber, Max. From <u>Max Weber: Essays in Sociology</u>. ed. by H.H. Gerth and C. Wright Mills. New York: Oxford University Press, 1946.

Whyte, William. <u>The Organization Man</u>. New York: Simon and Schuster, 1956.

Willis, Gary. "The Kennedy Imprisonment," <u>The Atlantic Monthly</u>, January-February, 1982.

Wittgenstein, Ludwig. <u>Philosophical Investigations</u>. New York: MacMillan Publishing Co., Inc., 1958.